WHAT PEOPLE ARE SAYING ABOUT

LIVING LIGHTLY: A JOURNEY THROUGH CHRONIC ~~~ M.E.)

Jenny Light ha___ ___ ___ nic Fatigue
Syndrome, as t___ ns given to
it. Having liv___ rough her
experience, her___ an inward
journey to ful___ ercises and
therapies that ___ ___ ___ used to overcome Chronic Fatigue
Syndrome.

Jan de Vries, Author of 42 nature cure books

I used VegEPA, an evening primrose and omega supplement
specifically for CFS/M.E. as part of my recovery process. Igennus
are endorsing me and I am endorsing their product as part of a
case study.

Igennus, Manufacturer

Living Lightly:
a journey through Chronic Fatigue Syndrome (M.E.)

Living Lightly:
a journey through
Chronic Fatigue
Syndrome (M.E.)

Jenny Light

AYNI
BOOKS

Winchester, UK
Washington, USA

First published by Ayni Books, 2015
Ayni Books is an imprint of John Hunt Publishing Ltd., Laurel House, Station Approach,
Alresford, Hants, SO24 9JH, UK
office1@jhpbooks.net
www.johnhuntpublishing.com
www.ayni-books.com

For distributor details and how to order please visit the 'Ordering' section on our website.

ISBN: 978 1 78535 139 6
Library of Congress Control Number: 2015937450

A CIP catalogue record for this book is available from the British Library.

Design: Lee Nash

Printed and bound by CPI Group (UK) Ltd, Croydon, CR0 4YY

We operate a distinctive and ethical publishing philosophy in all
areas of our business, from our global network of authors to
production and worldwide distribution.

CONTENTS

Foreword   xii

Acknowledgements   xiii

Introduction   xiv

Part 1 Collapse   1

1.   My collapse   3

2.   Cracks started to show!   11

3.   Loss of freedoms   19

4.   Cloud gazing   25

Part 2 Coping with Chronic Fatigue Syndrome   33

5.   Grounding, discharging and cleansing   35

6.   Coping with conversation and public places   45

7.   Psychic protection   51

8.   Sensitivity to sound and ELF (extremely low frequencies
     of electromagnetic energy)   59

9.   Pleasing other people   69

10. Coping with others' mixed reactions   81

11. The raw food diet   93

12. Getting a good sleep   101

13. Arrhythmia: the message of the heart   109

Part 3 Recovery and forging a healthier approach to life   115

14. Meaning of the illness   117

15. Acceptance   127

16. Other therapies and supplements   135

17. Ahimsa (non-violence): getting the balance right   143

18. A better way to be   151

Appendix A: My favourite raw food recipes   159
Appendix B: 14-day sleep diary   163
Bibliography   164
About the author   166

Through the clarity of time
We see our life mapped out
In colours, red and gold:
Experience etching our soul
Into a softness which
We couldn't have fathomed before.
I see a gentler way to be
And am more happy being me.

I dedicate this book to my mother, Jan, and daughters, Ashley and Lesley, who looked after me at my lowest ebb with Chronic Fatigue Syndrome. Without their unerring practical and emotional support, I would not have been able to take the first steps to recovery.

Also, this book is dedicated to all those suffering with extreme energy sensitivity and fatigue:

May this book lead you to full health and may you know your own inner light.

Foreword

There are a vast amount of books on Chronic Fatigue Syndrome/ M.E., including my own.

Living Lightly is a different book altogether. At first I thought 'Not another one!' until I picked it up, started to read it and couldn't put it down because this book is totally different from any others on the subject.

We can quickly see that Jenny Light has got a 'light' on the problem of Chronic Fatigue Syndrome, as there are many mysterious explanations given to it. Having lived with this condition herself, through her experience, her fight and research, Jenny takes you on an inward journey to full health, through healthy living, exercises and therapies that can be used to overcome Chronic Fatigue Syndrome much more quickly.

I was greatly impressed with this book, which I am sure will give many fellow sufferers of Chronic Fatigue Syndrome hope that this debilitating condition can be fought and won!

I wish Jenny every success with her book.

Jan de Vries
Jan de Vries Health Care Ltd
20 Wellington Square
Ayr
Ayrshire KA7 1EZ
Scotland, UK
www.jandevrieshealth.co.uk

Acknowledgements

I am deeply grateful to my guides and angels for carrying my spirit through the empty waste I felt inside to guiding me to place each word of this book.

I am indebted to my friend Anita Neilson, who, being a colleague with the same condition, grew to be my best friend and worked valiantly with each chapter as I wrote it and led herself back to health.

To my good friend Frank Murphy, a big thank-you for your spiritual healing and giving me the courage and energy to face myself on the inward journey to health.

To Neil Campbell, my deepest yoga friend and confidant, a big thank-you for proofreading my book and encouraging me on my inner journey.

To my grandchildren, Lily, Tom, Sandy, Elsie and Alice, thank you for your exuberance and joy in living that lifted my spirits and reminded me of joy on those days when I felt low.

And to my friends and clients who encouraged me along the way by giving positive feedback that this book was needed and was helpful to them.

I am grateful to Jan de Vries, naturopath, friend of the family and eminent author, for endorsing my book.

Introduction

It is with deepest gratitude to my illness that I write this book. That may seem strange, but without Chronic Fatigue Syndrome (CFS), I would not have experienced the magical teachings it had in store for me.

I would like to take you on my journey. It doesn't matter whether you have suffered Chronic Fatigue Syndrome, post-viral fatigue, myalgic encephalomyelitis (M.E.) or not, I hope my journey will be entertaining and that you, my reader, may gain some insights into yourself. This book is for you. You, who just happened to pick up this book, if you believe in the coincidence. For my part, I believe that I was meant to have Chronic Fatigue, that I was meant to learn from it, and that you, dear reader, were meant to share in what I have learned. This book is not dedicated to associating with symptoms or disease labels. There are plenty of other books on the subject. This book instead leads you to associating with wellness by helping you to embark on your own journey of self-enquiry and giving you the tools to heal yourself along the way.

Each chapter is designed to lead you through the process of your own self-healing by empowering you to spiritually grow from this experience. You will learn how to connect with the earth's core, with your higher self, use prayer and develop gratitude and acceptance. The chapters conclude with a powerful affirmation which you can write out and repeat over and over several times a day. I suggest that you take your time to learn the tools from each chapter and record your healing journey. I promise that when you take responsibility for your own healing process, you will not be the person you were before. You will be more fully you, more whole as you step through all the lessons of your condition.

So sit back and prepare for our journey. This moment now is a new moment: fresh and poignant with all possibilities. Take a deep breath in and breathe out the past.

Visualise a shining white light coming down from your highest self through your crown. Breathe in white light; breathe grey out to the trees outside.

Keep breathing in white into your heart and breathing out the grey until you feel fresher and clearer at your core.

Now you are ready. With a sense of expectancy, like a child at Christmas, turn the page...

Part 1

Collapse

Chapter 1

My collapse

There was a time when my own family had to have appointments to see me in my busy schedule. I was busier than Job. I used to say to people that I burned my candle at both ends and four places in the middle! I was even proud of the fact.

And I liked to help everyone. The saying: 'If you want something done, ask a busy person', was never truer. And I couldn't say no to anyone who asked. It was as if I was playing a game of pride with myself to see how much I could do in one day, stretching the bounds of what was humanly possible. Every 10 minutes I had spare, I'd fill with one task or another. I took multi-tasking to a new level: I'd use the moments when I should have been overseeing my food cooking to practise piano, wash out a bin or sew a cushion. Needless to say, I often burned my pot dry when I got absorbed in another task, or two! But that was part of the buzz for me: to see how much I could fit in, like I was cheating time itself or at the very least, beating myself. It was as if I had a personal bet with myself to complete two tasks before the food burned. Not surprising I didn't always get it right. Nor did I think that I'd ever burn my own pot dry.

Perhaps it's my competitive nature that's partly to blame? Choosing to be in the teaching profession was also an indicator: teachers are control freaks who take planning and preparation to the *nth* degree. It's a prerequisite of the job which suited my 'A type' personality. It's of no surprise to see that Chronic Fatigue Syndrome and M.E. are really prevalent among teachers. At the time, I mused that my colleagues who purported to suffer from M.E. or CFS were a bit pathetic, or dare I say it, maybe attention seeking? You never think that it'll happen to you. As time has gone on, I have learned never to judge anyone else: 'There but for the grace of god go I.'

I suppose, looking back, I had an indication within myself that the energy output needed to maintain a high achievement rate was too great. But I was burning fast, like a rocket, an adrenalin junkie…it felt so good to be 'doing' all the time. I felt high. Important. Like others might respect me better? I certainly respected myself best when I was achieving.

I was a 'lists person'. My list of things to do being systematically ticked off gave me great pleasure. Looking back, it's a sad kind of achievement. But immersed in it, I felt important, infallible, a success. But underlying it all, the toll was being marked up against this unachievable, non-existent goal I was setting myself.

When the cracks started to show, I didn't recognise them as warning signs: At my lunch break, I'd be puzzled that my arm shook so much bringing my fork to my mouth from a plate on my lap. I learned to tense my arm so food didn't fall off or so that others didn't notice (how concerned are we to appear capable and normal to others?). And then there were the cases of flu which I got, bringing an overheated brain, foggy thought processes, sore bones and sometimes a fever. What was also odd was that often I was the only person going down with flu. Why was that? I seemed to get this with a worrying frequency, which increased the more rundown I became as the school year ran on. January, February and March were the lowest months.

The holidays became vital to my recovery in order to start afresh, especially the summer months. However, 10 years ago, in the year that I turned 40, for the first time in my life I hit a wall. My marriage had broken down, I had moved into a new place on my own, I had health issues with fibroids causing heavy bleeding, lots of visits to gynaecology, a new relationship and I was concurrently working hard in the evenings after work and at weekends for a Chartered Teacher award. I had never experienced feeling burnt out before. My body had previously been a capable, tireless machine which would perform anything I wanted it to. I hadn't really thought about it or really appreciated it. Like a well-running car, you don't notice it. It's when it starts to speak to you in the voice of tiredness, when even after 9 or 10 hours' sleep you never seem to feel rested – that and the awful dislocated feeling of not being quite present in the proceedings. That was the first time that I realised something was wrong. Other people assured me that it was just my age catching up with me. My mother assured me that she'd hit the same wall at 40 after completing her honours degree, so I took it as a temporary glitch. If I rested up a while, then I'd be able to take up the reins again. Surely? So, I remember speaking to my boss to ask her not to set me up for any further training courses or CPD (continuing professional development) for a year.

However, me being me, it wasn't long before exciting new projects came to me and, you guessed it, I couldn't say no. Not that I wanted to say no. As far back as I can remember, I've always had a zest for life and immersing myself in creative projects, a spark which I shared with my younger sister. As children, she and I would beaver away on craft projects together by designing, sewing, knitting and building ideas that came to us. My mother encouraged us and kept a 'make-it' box full of waste boxes, paper and assorted junk for our projects. As we had very little money, we learned to be inventive. One time, in order to make an outfit for a wedding, I spent a prized 50p on fabric dye, to dye an old sheet to make into a long skirt onto which I sewed a chiffon frill (from an old scarf of my mum's), and I designed a herringbone belt laced at the waist in stiffened chiffon. My top was an old white jumper which I cut off at the underarms, turned it upside down so that the rib at the waist was now across my chest and used the sleeves for the hem and the straps. I wove my shoulder bag from strips of waste fabric, leaving long fringes of cloth hanging and attached a plaited strap. So the whole outfit cost me 50p! I got a great thrill out of thrift and inventiveness. I'm a fastidious worker and was most keen for anything I made not to look 'home-made'. This aspect of my character has been both a bugbear and a blessing. Sometimes, I could have got away with not quite putting in so much effort but I could always see the flaws (seams not lined up exactly, not well cut, lines not straight...). So I worked harder than I should have perhaps at everything. My sister's style was a lot looser and flowing but she seemed to produce craft items with flair...I just credited her as being the real artist here and I was only a good copyist, except when it came to dressmaking – that was my forte. It was no surprise to anyone when I set up my own dressmaking business after I graduated from Glasgow University.

Personal drive and motivation to achieve well for myself but to be recognised for my achievements too are my hallmarks. I take after my grandmother in this respect, who pulled herself from poverty and diphtheria into social status and wealth. She remained organised, problem-solving and thrifty to her death, a few years ago, at 94 years. Even as her body was failing her, she didn't get down-hearted but just remarked 'Well, I wonder, how can I get round this?' I respected her attitude to the changing demands which life placed on her and that she was indomitable to the last.

So with my own illness, I apply her approach: what can I make of the turn of events for me now? I believe that there is no coincidence, that I drove myself to illness over many years of not listening to my body, not choosing to pay heed to the tell-tale signs. Although, in my own defence, I neither recognised the signs for what they were nor had any will to do anything any differently than I was doing. Well, hell mend me. And it did. My own personal hell ensued.

That March 2010, I woke on the fateful day of my collapse and had difficulty thinking clearly. I had run 17 twilight courses for teachers end on to the school day between September and March, in addition to my daytime teaching post. And I was also secretary of a local environment group on a voluntary basis, giving up many hours of my time a week. I was burnt out. I had spoken to my boss the previous week saying I was stressed and asking for help to set up the IT, which she dismissed by saying 'Well, everyone else manages.' With that comment, I continued to deny what I was feeling; otherwise I would have been a failure to myself and my colleagues if I hadn't been able to cope. As I was later to realise, this need to prove oneself capable at all costs was key to understanding Chronic Fatigue Syndrome.

So there I was, the morning after running yet another course, waking feeling disconnected from the world around me, trying to process a simple choice like what clothes to wear. Normal tasks become cloudy and onerous when your thoughts won't work. I caught sight of myself in a mirror as I perched on the end of the bed, half dressed, and was struck by my ghastly pallor. Hands clasped either side of my face I spoke to my reflection, saying 'I don't feel well.' My reflection just stared back with glassy eyes that were too shiny to be healthy but didn't take charge and tell me to phone in sick. Unable to make any worthwhile decisions it was easier to roll along with the time-honoured habits. So with difficulty, I managed to dress myself, still thinking this would pass as I drove the 30 minutes to the school. I was aware of a fog in my brain while driving and nearly turned round for home more than twice. But what creatures of habit we are. We seek to fulfil duty unless the situation is dire. Funny thing is, when your thoughts are so foggy, your normal processing of what's dire, when to pack it in, or when to rest doesn't work. All that remains is this automaton, religiously, robotically attempting to go on with the primary mission, even in the face of sense or reason. Even when the primary mission should be overridden to one of self-preservation, you don't notice.

So I went on that morning, until break time, trying to appear as normal. All of my mental processing going into a façade of normality when all the while I felt a gnawing sense of unease and unreality, through a foggy tunnel, distant from the proceedings, clock-watching until break. And at break time, that's what I did – I broke down, crying to the head teacher, who could see I wasn't well, as any normal person would have, and sent me home. My GP (general practitioner/family doctor) that afternoon labelled it 'Stress' and offered me antidepressants which I declined. Even in my fogged state I knew I wasn't depressed. This was something else. Clutching my 4-week sick note, I went home to rest.

Rest doesn't describe the complete collapse which ensued. I was so low that I had to lie flat for weeks. Even lifting my head or going to the toilet were strenuous tasks. The heart beating inside my chest was sore, and breathing too was a great physical effort. My live-in partner at the time just said, 'I told you you were doing too much.' I regarded this as an unhelpful statement from a man who had employed a strategy of withdrawal from helping out in the house in order to force me into slowing down over the previous months. It didn't take a genius to work out that this would only give me more to do. Well, something inside me snapped and I thought, 'Well! Hung for a sheep as for a lamb' (a wonderful phrase which relates to the death penalty for stealing livestock: if your neck is on the line, you might as well make it worthwhile!) and asked him to leave. So within 1 week I collapsed, signed off ill indefinitely and ended a relationship which had been sour for over a year. Double whammy.

Luckily, I have a family who rallied round to help feed me and look after me. My body felt mortally heavy as every movement or thought tired me, and sent me reeling one step forward, four steps back. It felt like I was wading in tar at the bottom of a barrel because any movement was an extreme effort. What was worse was that feeling of being dead inside me. I had no energy to engage emotionally with the world. There was no joy or rest in my wracked body. Without my mother's and daughters' support and care over the many months it took for me to focus on rest and healing, I would still be at the bottom of that barrel. Extricating myself out of the sludge of tar coating the base of that barrel became my only goal.

You just never think that it'll be you. Lying there gave me lots of opportunities to look back and reflect. Would I do anything differently? What was the point of all this creative zeal and zest for life if you had to limit what brings you joy? And isn't 'Regret' a waste of precious energy? A dragging, sucking pull-down into the tar barrel, where you could wallow? So I realised that I didn't want to wallow. I had done exactly what I wanted with my life and nor would I have done anything differently. And in this too, I would use this breakdown to my greater wisdom and benefit. I had lots to learn from it. With this positive mindset, I'm not sure whether it was despite or because of the physical challenge I was now experiencing, I set about engaging with my new state to find out where it would lead me.

That's when wonderful words would appear in my head which, when I was able to pick up a pen, flowed out as poetry, a process like letting blood which stemmed from me without thought and pumped forth onto the page. I could clearly hear words being dictated to me to write. Words of wonder, comfort, joy. Words expressing melancholy but also words of hope. I knew without doubt that this situation which I was experiencing would bring me great wisdom if I were prepared to face myself fully and unashamedly. Indeed, I believe that we have nothing to be ashamed of. We are all developing wisdom through living our lives. A wisdom which grows from each encounter with ourselves, if we acknowledge the truth within us. God isn't judging us. It is only us who are. God knows that growing involves sometimes making unwise choices so that we can choose a wiser choice next time.

I found it really helpful to keep a journal to chart my healing progress. I suggest that you acquire a new notebook which is dedicated to recording your healing process. It's helpful to just let the pen flow. If you engage in a dialogue with yourself, you might be amazed with the insights you'll open up. Allow your body to 'speak' to you and write its responses.

You can record how 'light' you feel each morning. I used a smiley face system in the margin for an at-a-glance record of my energy levels each day: a big smile for a day with lots of energy; a flat-line smile for a day when I felt a bit flat; a sad face for a day when I was laid low with fatigue. This easy record helped me to recognise what strategies helped me and to pinpoint which activities or events were not conducive to healing my condition. So I was able to see over time that, even when it didn't feel like it, I was gradually improving.

Happy writing!

Affirmation:
'I allow myself to have complete rest.'

Chapter 2

Cracks started to show!

I'd like to say that life was easy before my collapse. That every-thing had a place and a place for everything. But there wasn't perfection. Far from it. Indeed, it was the undercurrent of imper-fection that was rippling through into my life that caused the breakdown.

But I get ahead of myself. Externally, I had everything that I needed: a fabulous career where I was respected, two healthy, talented daughters, a husband who provided for us, a comfortable home, a yoga class with students who looked up to me, and many other talents. I even thought to myself that I was happy.

The undercurrent of anger that ran through my life, I chose to overlook: if I didn't address it, it would cease to exist. In other words, I was denying myself. And the anger just would not go away. The older I got, coming up on my fortieth birthday, the louder my internal anger got. It even developed a sound and a voice. The internal scream, like the famous painting by Edvard Munch, grew and grew to fever pitch, the less I refused to acknowledge it. In company, I was afraid that if anyone came too close, they'd even hear the sound emanating from my head. How can a sound be so overwhelming and anyone else not hear it? That's the strange separatist nature of existence that I don't understand. I know that spiritually we're all linked through the Oneness of God, so why couldn't others sense my scream? But the strange thing is my family have subsequently told me that they didn't know what I was going through because I didn't speak. How can my exterior be so calm and so false as to belie my inner world and no-one else knew? Don't get me wrong. I would have been appalled if anyone *had* known about my inner struggle – I was so hell bent (interesting choice of words, Jenny) on appearing calm and in control. And also *being* in control of myself and situations around me. Naively, I thought that if I maintained external control I would have mastery over my internal struggle and it would all resolve itself. But it just wouldn't lie down and sit quiet.

Have you ever tried meditating? Any book will tell you the whole purpose is about control of the mind. The mind is likened to trying to steer a chariot where all four horses are wilfully pulling in different directions and your job is to pull them into line through gargantuan mastery of your will. And this was my approach: a forceful, internal opposition to my wayward self. And so I was fighting myself and denying that my emotions had any part to play: they were simply an annoyance in the goal of self-mastery. At the time, I didn't realise that the way to mastery wasn't to deny part of yourself – it is only through loving, really loving, all aspects of yourself that you can find an inner peace. But I didn't know that then. So there I was in inner turmoil. Getting up every day and filling every waking moment with chores, people to care for and things to do. It's true, the busier you are, the less time you have to think and reflect.

Things were steadily breaking down between my husband and me over a period of several years. The final straw for me came on our last holiday together. Ironically, we had what we'd dreamed of for a while, a holiday abroad on our own, as our musical daughters were away touring America and Canada with the Fiddle Orchestra. Perhaps it was the absence of my children which highlighted to me so clearly that my husband wasn't who I wanted to be with. I realised how deeply unhappy I was in the relationship and my internal scream took on a new voice, loudly and incessantly saying: 'I don't want to be with this man! I don't want to *be* with this man!' again and again. I'd brought a book to sit beside the hotel pool and read but the words were so insistent and emphatic that I couldn't hear myself read. So I sat and unwound in the warm sunshine and saw myself clearly for the first time without my familiar distractions or chores or children to take care of. And I looked over at my husband and felt sorry for him because my life with him had to end. He was like a familiar stranger lying there: why was I with him? Any of the reasons and the story of my life receded into the annals of history and in that moment I knew I had nothing in common with this man any more. Our life had run its course and I was being drawn to move on without him.

But I didn't say any of this to him. I didn't have the courage to speak – what if my thoughts were just a momentary blip, a flash of madness, and I ruined things by speaking? So my life resumed back home until the fateful night in December (why is it always December, the darkest month of the year?) when I stood in our kitchen with him and I knew it was over.

I always wonder why pivotal moments in our life come without portent. You expect somehow that you might wake up that morning and just know that it was going to be a momentous day. But I didn't. My day started off as any other without alarm bells ringing to warn me. So there I was standing in my kitchen with this stranger whom I knew better than anyone and, quite clearly, I felt a warm hand on my shoulder and the disembodied kind words in my ear, 'Go Jenny. Go now.' You might think this could have been scary since it was only he and I in the room but strangely it wasn't. I felt a deep calm come over me and I told him quietly that I had to leave. It is to his credit that he took this very well and even helped me carry my few bags out to our car. I told him that I'd be staying at my mother's house for a while. But as soon as I drove away, I suddenly felt a weight lift off me and I knew I'd never be back.

I'm telling you this because it was an important lesson for me to learn. That I had thought when I was unhappy in my marriage that I had to blame someone else, namely him, for all the problems so I could have a reason to end our marriage. That if only he was more x, y or z, that I would be happy. But it came to me. I didn't need to blame him to have reasons to justify leaving. Simply being unhappy was reason enough. Blame wasn't necessary. Being unhappy within me was both the message and the justification.

So from that point I knew I had to be true to myself, I had to do what makes *me* happy. That's what I'd like to say to you. Don't waste years of your life berating someone's bad points, which, anyway, is pointless because we can't change others. Nor should we try because we are not responsible for anyone except ourselves (unless they are small children). Whatever irritation, blame, anger etc you send towards someone is mirrored back to you by the cosmic Law of Reflection. So you are really only running yourself down in berating another, since what you give out you get back magnified.

We can, however, change ourselves. It is ultimately more worthwhile pitching your focus into changing yourself because it really works: you are a self-determined human being. How you determine, or programme yourself, is how you will experience life.

That is the journey of this book. We embark on a journey of self-exploration and learn how to work on the deep healing required to be truly non-reactive when your buttons are pressed. And to do what makes you happy.

I suggest that you take time to reflect here on your goals and aspirations. What if being ill was your body bringing you a message?

Is there something you really want to do with your life?
Have you an unfulfilled desire or a burning wish?
Are you doing what you always wanted?
Do your relationships serve you?
So what's holding you back?
Be prepared to look very closely at yourself. Look for the small annoyance or tightness inside yourself where you feel anger or where you don't express your truth. This repressed feeling is actually your key to change.

You may wish to take time here to ponder your responses to these questions and write your feelings in your journal.

You may feel that your condition renders you powerless. I wish to impress on you that this feeling is not the truth and that when you acknowledge why it has happened and take charge of your own healing, you will feel your power again. This is a temporary phase in your healing process.

It is essential that you learn how to self-heal by linking with your inner essence. This is done by simply laying hands on your abdomen and connecting both to the earth and your higher self. This incarnation on earth is a free-will zone so our higher vibrational helpers, such as guides and angels, will not interfere with our free will. We need to ask for help in order for it to be given to us. Repeat 'Thank you' three times after your appeal, believing that you have already received what you are asking for. Saying 'So be it, Amen' seals the prayer through the power of Divine Will and ensures that you will receive it.

Practising self-healing

Lie quietly and imagine a lightning rod from your tailbone or feet travelling down into the earth. Allow all pain, tension, others' energies or anxieties to flow down and discharge into the earth.

Place your hands on the area of tightness you can feel in the body which reflects trapped emotion.

Then ask for help to release the tightness from your guardian angel, God, archangels or ascended masters. My prayer usually starts:

> *'I hereby call on my healing guides and helpers, my guardian angel and all seven archangels: Gabriel, Raphael, Jophiel, Michael, Chamuel, Zadkiel and Uriel, to take this tension from my body, heal me and fill me full of love and light. Thank you, thank you, thank you. It is done. Amen.'*

Then breathe in through your hands into the area in need of releasing. Visualise yourself letting go and handing over the tightness to the angels to transmute. Feel the release and how much lighter you feel. Visualise white light pouring into your body.

Use an affirmation such as 'I am totally healthy' and repeat it three times.

Imagine yourself cloaked in a protective blanket, which covers your head and curls under your feet. Express gratitude for the help and support you've received. Focus on the feeling of gratitude and thankfulness. Become aware of the outer world returning to your consciousness.

Please be mindful that old ways of being may take several healing sessions to shift and release because our attachment to reacting in a certain way has become ingrained over time, possibly several lifetimes. I know that this task of self-healing is possible. How do I know that? Because you are facing yourself every moment of every day, as I was, like a suspended animation, until you do face yourself. Once you realise that it is all up to you, that's when the healing journey truly starts. And I believe that you are more than up to the challenge. Blessings on your uniquely wonderful journey.

Affirmation:
'I am totally healthy.'

I feel deeply as the waters close over my head
There is no going back
Only suffocating sink,
Murky waters obscure.
Where is the peace?
Where the safe haven in strife?
Heart sore and head hung,
Peace abandons, wild seas,
A smattering of rain in a squall.
Seas rising swallow as Jonah,
Deep inside the belly of the ocean
Where turbulence quiets:
Dark depths have their own calm.
If I let go, I sink.
No care, caress or hapless soldiering on,
Peace at last in the quiet deep of myself.

Chapter 3

Loss of freedoms

There is a terrible sense of loss of freedoms with Chronic Fatigue Syndrome. Things that you previously could do, you now can't. All those joyful hours planning new ventures or following pleasurable pursuits: curtailed. And now it is just tiring to think about it. One feels a mix of anger, frustration and grief. At its worst, the world narrows around you to the bed you're occupying and the four walls around you.

It's a major excursion to visit the toilet and navigate back to lie prone in bed, while the world spins around. The yawning gap of the stairwell as I passed seemed ready to swallow me whole if I should topple, so I tried not to look. The longer I was vertical, the more likely I was to be hit with waves of nausea and dizziness before I could make it back to the bed. So the bathroom was a bit of a hit-and-run affair to get back to lying down as quickly as possible. The length of time to return to equilibrium after this mammoth effort well exceeded the action.

Here is an extract from my diary at my lowest ebb:

I am trying to think through a fog. My head is too hot, actually hot to touch. It's as if my brain is burning up. Burnt out? Done too much again it seems. Such a fine line to tread. I wish I could get it right. Nearly there a lot of the time for I can see progress, if I look back these months.

But still today, time is passing in the oddest manner for I feel dislocated and not quite here. Choosing which clothes to put on today is a huge effort of focus. My usual order of dressing, out of the window. So I just grab the first thing my hand falls on until this clears.

I have two things to attend to today...feels like a

mountain, or rather two, that I have to traverse. Scramble up them or call off? I am seriously contemplating calling off the first – but there I go again disappointing and letting others down, again! So very hard.

My brain can't think what to do. Another sign of the fatigue. Thoughts won't come easily to any decision. It's like living in a dream, only it's a waking dream where I can't wake up to normal consciousness.

So I hit the shower. The one thing I know which often works. Cool, wet hair cools my head and reduces the heat in my brain. But today this isn't working. Still it's early. It's only 11.30am. I tell myself, I am usually OK by mid-afternoon. Sit and wait. Patience, Jenny. You know it passes.

So I learned to lie still and reflect on the past. What a colourful life to have led! So many wonderful places, sights, smells and people to share your journey with, which Fortune grants the good health to enjoy. The world shines when you are healthy, with a shining spirit and a zest for life. Lying prone, there is still zest but the body doesn't feel fit to jump and do as it was bid. In fact, even pondering my past escapades engaged my beating heart, endorphins and adrenalin kicked in and it tired my body to think! The body responds to each thought as if it were occurring in the present moment: a fear response to fight or flight or a joyful response to action. Planning an action in your head, your body responds as if it was actually doing it, instead of merely thinking about it.

So you learn to lie quietly and still your thoughts; to bring them to rest in the present moment. You learn that the longer you can lie still and quiet, the more recharged your energy levels will be. So bring your thoughts to rest on any ease of comfort in the body (even with a body in pain, there will be ease or comfort somewhere). What you focus on increases, so focus on ease or pleasure, not the dis-ease. Breathe peace into your beating heart, slow the breath. Focus on the comfort of clean, smooth bedding.

Focus on the quiet around you. Noises and voices in the street may take your mind away from calm and you may start to imagine the scene outside your window. So you learn to disengage and let the sounds filter through and away without attaching thought or emotion, without engaging with the sound. And the peace increases. You can hear the blood in your own head and the intensity of the beat of your heart, perhaps strong pulsing at the solar plexus which may even be visible through clothing. Notice how your body feels with detachment. Practise detachment.

So you learn to think *Peace*. Think *Ease*. Breathe in *peace* through your fingertips on the solar plexus. Then you learn to go beyond the physical body to the energy body beneath and beyond. You may notice the pulsing or oscillating energy body as palpably strong. You learn that '*smiling*' internally deepens and lengthens the oscillations or pulses, which transfers through into the physical body.

You learn that dis-ease, for I believe Chronic Fatigue Syndrome is an energetic 'dis ease', starts first of all in the energetic body, which maps itself over time into the physical body. Ask yourself how far back you knew something wasn't right, deep inside yourself, but you trundled on regardless? It's plain to me that the dis-ease within me started a long time ago, probably 10 years before I fell ill with Chronic Fatigue Syndrome, but I wasn't listening to the messages then.

Whatever you give attention to increases, so let's come back to the peace with a meditation on the inner pulsing of your life force. Let's create long, pure, fine emanations of light to ease the pulse within your physical frame. It's like learning to live to the beat of a different drum. Your soul drum, not the harsh beat of the world. Your life and healing depend on turning your life around at this pivotal point. And you can learn to bring your own finely tuned life force through into this physical world through your physical body.

This is the experience that you are participating in. How well you engage with your own healing process is determining your minute by minute experience. I suggest that you try this healing meditation once a day and bring your focus to being and *feeling* well, as your soul purpose at this time.

Meditation on the inner pulsing of your life force

Lie on your back and rest.

Place your hands on your abdomen. Bring your attention to breathing in and out.

Ask your angels and guardians to help bring you healing and to a state of calm and grace.

Focus on the fine-ness, the joy of who you are behind your physical body.

Smile internally. The smile radiates into your abdomen and down your legs. Ride the waves of this subtle peace.

Smile internally. The smile radiates across your chest, down your arms and back into your belly through your hands. Ride the deepening waves of peace.

Smile internally inside your skull. Light of subtle pure form radiates within your head, across your face, down your neck, inside your ears and filling your mouth and down into your shining body.

Lie peacefully smiling. Bask in the waves of healing grace.

Notice any small 'smiles' breaking out over your body, in your wrists, throat, eyes, ears.

Notice your heart opening.

Think PEACE, PEACE, PEACE as you ride these waves.

Think ALL WILL BE WELL. ALL IS WELL.

Focus on smiles and the wellness within you.

Be thankful for this opportunity to rest.

Accept all help graciously and with gratitude.

'Smile' a cloak of peace and protection from the harshness

of the world around your shoulders, covering your head and wrapping lovingly around your feet.

Try to keep this peaceful state of grace as you awake and engage with the world once more.

Affirmation:
'I am safe and at peace. All is well.'

Lazy clouds scud across the sun,
Spun in white light, each one.
No more do I spin my threads
As tired as I dream myself to be.
I sink down in my big white bed
Watching clouds with no effort,
transforming here and stretching there,
light breaking through in bright shafts
or bleeding around clouds in gold.
For I need be nothing or do nothing,
to perceive these aerial beauties.
And hour after hour, am absorbed
And healed by watching clouds.

Chapter 4

Cloud gazing

When I was at my lowest points, all interaction on any level was painful and tiring. Cloud gazing, however, became a really restful pursuit. When I was awake but had to lie out for those long hours of battery recharging, watching the changing moods of the sky was restorative.

It's when you are so low that thought itself is an effort, that you realise so profoundly that thoughts are always bubbling up. I felt like that fable about 'The Magic Salt-Mill' – an unstoppable churn of thoughts which just wouldn't stop coming, grinding away until all the sea was salt, or in this case until my energy was gone!

Cloud gazing on the other hand was a gentle pastime which gave my mind something to latch onto, while the rest of me got a chance to recharge. I liked to watch for the light bleeding through the clouds, for even on an overcast day there is still light coming through. I suppose I could have taken this as a hopeful metaphor, but really I just loved to 'soak up' the sunlight and found all its forms breaking round billows of cloud vapour a balm to my eyes and soul. No matter how despondent I felt about my demise or heavy or empty (which was worse – being too tired to have any feelings at all), staring up at the sky was restful and calming.

It brings back memories of staring out of the window at primary school at blue and white skies through the panes in the high windows of the Victorian building. Sometimes I zoned out of the proceedings to find rest in myself. I assumed everyone did that (you can't imagine that others perceive the world differently from how you do when you are a child). I realise that sky gazing is a recurring theme in my life: I used to lie flat on the lawn in our back garden or at my grandfather's farm watching clouds sweep across the sky, fascinated by how they assume different shapes and faces. Gestalt theory at its best, a psychologist would say. But they really do march across the sky like a procession of elephants or dinosaurs holding tails or dolphins flying! Or occasionally the face of God or an angel (so I imagine) appears. Those are the sublimely beautiful moments when my heart expands to greet the vision and I am flooded with a sense of grace.

Sometimes I close my eyes and let the bright sunlight filter through closed lids, watching coalescing auroras pulse in beautiful colours. On opening my eyes I could see motes of light sparkling in and out of existence, tiniest sparks dancing joyously in the sunlight. My dad once told me it was *prana*, life force itself, that I was witnessing and it made me feel special to have a dad who saw the world differently from all the other kids' dads. I was reminded that I was special, we were special. To see the world with spiritual eyes is a joy in itself.

So lying flat on my back, which is the only position I found which stopped the room spinning round, I got rest and again found myself watching clouds. Sometimes for 4 or 5 hours a day. When I voiced this to my GP, I could hear myself speaking like a mad person. Who watches clouds for 5 hours a day? Only people who need a secure asylum to watch the sky from! But it was true. Reading was impossible because my mind was required to focus and my brain was too fuzzy and hot to take in the squiggles of text on a page. TV and music were a barrage into my quiet world and an assault on my energy field. Conversation was tricky as I couldn't hold a train of thought in order to get out one sentence without intense effort; this was more difficult if I was also assaulted by the energy field of the person, if they were present. Short phone calls were bearable. But apart from that, I was alone in a quiet world with the skies. Only the sky gave me something to watch which didn't challenge me to change, interact or my mind to do anything except watch, like flickering candle images before my mind. Shapes appear and disappear within the frame of my bedroom window. Even on an overcast day, I could be entertained by the smudges of darker clouds with just a suggestion of light bleeding through, the interplay between the elements of air and water. I drank up the light like a drowning person clutching at the lifebuoy. I felt like I was being handed a boon which I needed.

Maybe it's because I'm an air sign that I find skies so attractive? Or maybe the wide open sky offered me escape from the physical lack of energy? A symbol of hope that all would be well? I only know that while my mind was occupied (note how I felt separate from the constant stirrings of my restless mind) I, the soul part of me, was able to receive valuable healing in soaking up the light. I noted the separatist nature of existence, that I was able to be aware of two states of being at once. Tricking my mind into being occupied freed me up to experience something else, something profound and healing.

While my physical eyes watched the light changing in the sky, my psychic eye and my pineal gland were on recharge: 5 hours and the world stopped spinning, my mind began to be able to focus a wee bit at a time. I'd sit up for a bit to see if I felt ready to rise, but often after ten minutes sitting up, I'd return to prone position as the room would start to spin again. And so my mornings and early afternoons would pass, with short forays to the bathroom or kitchen and back to bed to recover from these trips, lying flat in bed.

While this sounds depressing, I am not a depressive person. I would lie and ask myself: why is this happening to me? And the answers would come: because you need the rest. Because you need the time to reflect on your life, to regroup again with a clearer understanding of who you are. Because you need to experience peace.

I don't believe anyone is a victim. I believe that everything happens to us because we've something to learn from it.

So what did I learn?

That it takes a great effort and energy outlay to be the 'doing' person that I was.

That we can't be doing people 7 days a week, 365 days a year. A 2-week holiday doesn't recharge us from the constant barrage of experiences and expectations on us every day.

I found that I was not a robot: my machine, i.e. this body, needed rest. But more importantly, my soul needed rest. Life presents us with constant lessons on a daily, hourly, moment-to-moment basis. If we have no time to reflect then what are we learning? How to be automatons? To-keep-going-at-all-costs-no-matter-what- - - -? Like a hamster on a treadmill?

No, we are soul first, human second. And our soul needs reflection time to assimilate the experiences presented to us, that we create for ourselves. I realise why observance of a Sabbath day, a rest day, is really important. Not necessarily for religious reasons, but for spiritual reasons. A day of rest without all the usual distractions of shops, pubs, cinema or TV. Just think, if everyone were quiet on a Sunday, how restful that would be for us all; the ethers would be quiet as everyone stilled their minds in religious observance (if that's your thing) or in quiet reflection. Quieting of the buzz of thoughts in the town around you is really important to a sensitive like me. Imagine people taking rest and reflection seriously to think, what have I learned this week? Have I been acting and speaking as my highest good would act or speak? As I imagine God would act? How can I observe a better way to be me? Surely that's what an elevated society would do? It seems to me that what marks us as primitive is our need for constant distraction from ourselves.

So after many restorative months watching clouds, my advice is to take the time out. This time has been gifted to you for this rest and regrouping period. Be grateful for this well-earned rest. Perhaps you made an unconscious decision and gifted it to yourself? Perhaps this was all part of your plan before you were born? I would suggest that you make the most advantage of this time. When you are well, you may not get this block of quiet time again (and yes, I did say 'when you are well', for I firmly believe in your recovery to full health, if you are prepared to put in the work to help yourself). No magic pill from a third party here. Just you. Down time, just to experience the you of You. (Like Anna in the musical *The King and I*, in my mind I'm dancing with Yul Brynner singing *'Getting to know me...!'* Humour lifts my spirits even in the most depressive moments.)

Listen to the silence within yourself. Is there silence? Is there, in fact, a lot being told to you, that you are saying to yourself, in those quiet moments? What if you were to really ask those questions of yourself? Not 'Why me?' But simply, 'Why?'

I invite you to write this dialogue with yourself in your journal. Happy listening!

I would like to introduce you to the power of gratitude. Feeling grateful is the polar opposite of feeling depressed and a victim. Gratitude immediately opens up possibilities. It brings us to a state of hope. It also enables us to see that we are very fortunate. There is always something to be grateful for, even in our darkest times. The secret power of gratitude is that it helps us view the world totally positively and in so *doing we create the condition that we are feeling grateful for*. Link words, intention and a feeling of gratitude to create the magic. This is an alchemical secret which is now becoming known in public knowledge as we move into the new era in human evolution.

How to bring in the power of gratitude:

Can you find ten things to be grateful for, that your health condition has gifted you? There may be many negative outcomes but re-focus your attention on the positives.

Learning to tune in to the power of gratitude as a major turnaround (instead of regret or frustration). Perhaps you are learning patience? Your statement of gratitude could read:

'I am grateful that I am patient with others and myself.'

Perhaps you are grateful for the support you are receiving to help you heal and your affirmation could be:

'I am grateful for the healing support of (name) which helps me to _____.'

Perhaps you are finding a great deal of frustration with your limitations. In working with gratitude, the statement must be carefully chosen to be positively worded in the present tense, as if you already have the result you're looking for.

'I am grateful that I have unlimited energy so that I can ___ _____.'

Perhaps you may be experiencing dull or fuzzy thought processes. Word your statement of gratitude so that you create the quality you are wanting by using the Law of Attraction, to attract that quality to you.

Write your affirmation in the present tense as if it has

already been given to you. Attaching the emotional picture/feeling that you have already received what you desire, will send power to your affirmation.

'I am grateful to have clear and logical thoughts, which lets me _____.'

Write your ten affirmations based on your own thoughts and experiences.

Sit quietly with each one in turn. Say your affirmation three times (out loud or in your head), then seal the intent by saying 'Thank you' three times and then 'Amen, it is so.'

Feel the energy of gratitude flowing out of your heart. Visualise or tell yourself the scene of you telling a friend or family member that you have received your desired result. Try to 'feel' the emotion of the happiness pouring through.

Affirmation:
'I am grateful for _____.'

Part 2

Coping with Chronic Fatigue Syndrome

Chapter 5

Grounding, discharging and cleansing

When you are depleted in energy, you become aware of the effort that it takes to do the smallest tasks. Resting quietly on your own is the way to restoration. Every part of your being seeks rest and respite from people, well-meaning though they may be. Any conversation can be exhausting. Your bedroom is your safe haven and quiet space from worldly intrusion. In chapter 8, I describe ways of ensuring that your bedroom is a contamination-free zone. But for now, I support you in resting to recharge your energy 'battery'. So lie down and use the meditation in chapter 3 to withdraw into your peace-filled state.

Any excursion or conversation may involve you coming back with a little of another's energy. Without you being conscious of it or until you are conscious of it. You may just be aware that you feel very tired. Part of your energy field is wide open as a dumping ground. Other people may feel good around you but leave you feeling as if you have gone ten rounds with Mike Tyson.

Our main energetic exchanges beyond the physical body are through the chakras or energy wheels which relate to our energy bodies. Seen with higher vision, chakras look like many-petalled flowers, in beautiful, flowing, bright colours, which are situated at specific points along the main vertical energy channel running through the spine and head. Each vibrates at a different colour frequency, like the colours of a rainbow.

Red	Base chakra – points downwards from the base of the spine
Orange	Sacral chakra – opens to the front and back just above the pubic bone
Yellow	Solar Plexus chakra – opens to the front and back from the navel
Green	Heart chakra – opens to the front and back at the heart
Blue	Throat chakra – opens to the front and back at the pit of the throat
Deep blue	Brow chakra – opens to the front and back of the head, above and between the eyes
Violet or White	Crown chakra – opens upwards as a thousand petals

Each chakra also correlates to a specific endocrine gland. This is an important element in understanding the nature of illness and recovery to full health. Some chakras may be closed or blocked due to an earlier physical or emotional injury, which may have resulted in childhood or adolescence or continued from a previous incarnation. It would be helpful for you to be able to 'feel' into each chakra and scan whether it is a cleanly open energy centre or whether it has blockages which feel like tightness or appear dark when seen with inner sight. It does not matter whether you can see or visualise the chakras but we can all feel into them and how well they feel to be working.

Chakra energy body scan
Feel into your base chakra with its red flower opening between the legs from the perineum. Visualise the vibrant red colour. Is it healthy and strong? This is our main connection with the earth and this incarnation.

Feel into your sacral chakra which has an orange flower opening 3 or 4 fingers' width above the pubic bone. It has a root which extends out the other side of the spine. Can you feel this chakra? Does it glow a bright orange or it is dull?

Feel into your solar plexus which is 3 or 4 fingers' width above your navel. It has a glowing yellow flower, like the sun. Try to feel or see if this is healthy and open. Or does it feel tight and closed?

Feel into your heart chakra which is a many-petalled green flower rooted in the centre of your chest, behind the physical heart. Are all the petals open? Can you feel through your heart? Is it easy to imagine the bright green colour like fresh grass? Are you open behind the heart too?

Feel into the throat chakra which is a small blue flower at the base of the throat. Can you feel or see it opening? Is it a vibrant blue of a cloudless sky on a sunny day? Or does it feel dull and restricted? How do you feel at the back of the throat?

Feel into the brow chakra, situated between and slightly above the brows. It looks like two indigo blue petals opening across the forehead. Can you imagine 'seeing' through this chakra? Is the colour vibrant? Can you feel out of the back of your head, opening into the space behind you?

Feel into your crown chakra which is thousand-petalled like a lotus flower. Can you feel/see your whole crown opening as if your skin were being peeled back to allow your purple light to shine up out of the body? This is our main connection with our higher self and the Godhead. How bright is the light emanating from your crown?

Visualise yourself gently closing each flower, one by one.

Imagine that you are safe within a protective golden ball as you bring yourself back to waking consciousness.

This chakra scan is intended to help you gain insight into your own psychic anatomy. Please write your observations on each chakra in your journal. It might be beneficial to select one chakra at a time and sit within it and write your feelings/insights.

After your scan, I suggest that you revisit each chakra with the focus on sending healing light and 'charging' up the colour of each chakra. It is helpful to lay your hands on the area of each chakra in turn while asking for healing from your guides and the angels.

This book will work with the primary seven chakras but there are actually many more chakras which some of you may be aware of. We will explore more about the energy give-and-take between people through the chakras and our auric fields in chapter 6. We will deal with various methods of psychic protection, such as shielding chakras, in chapter 7. But for now you will learn how to ground and 'discharge' that unwanted energy which you've picked up, down into the earth.

Grounding is vital to recovery from a fatigue-based illness. We all have an energetic link, a cord of connection from our base energy wheel or *chakra* to the planet Earth below us. This cord links us when we decide to incarnate here. It keeps us 'grounded' and helps us to connect with our life purpose.

Grounding cord into the earth

Sit or lie comfortably but with awareness.

Breathe in and sigh out into the chair or bed below you.

Imagine that you have a lightning rod extending from your tailbone, down through the floor and deep into the earth beneath you.

Run another two grounding cords down through your legs, opening the small chakras at the back of your knees, the ankles and the soles of your feet, then into the ground. Imagine all three grounding cords entwining together and connecting you to the earth with a gentle suction down towards the centre of the Earth.

The suction on your grounding cords pulls any unwanted energy clear from your body and at the same time seeks to ensure that you are firmly connected with planet Earth.

Feel your energetic connection to the Earth through this

cord. Feel your connection to the pulsing heart of the planet. Hold this focus until you start to feel energy rising from Mother Earth in response to your connection.

Feel/see the energy from the Earth filling you with pure, white, healing light.

Sit within this healing space.

Offer up your gratitude to Mother Earth.

Imagine you have a golden cloak draped around your shoulders and tucked under your feet, with a loose hood over your head and face.

Let's look at the reasons why you are not well grounded. I have found that this is common in those suffering energetic dis-ease. They tend to have a poor association with their base chakra and a poor ability to remain grounded. At some point in your early development, you may not have properly developed this planetary link. This could be due to a reluctance to be incarnated, an injury to your coccyx, a difficulty in your early relationship to your parents, abuse or to lack of physical nurturing as a child.

I recognise that when I was younger, I didn't want to be here. I found Earth to be too hard, harsh and hurtful. My habitual response was to escape out of the top of my head and to spiral in the ethers where I felt free and I didn't have to engage with anyone. I zoned out and stared into 'space', engaging instead with the vast space above me. Then I discovered meditation and loved the control I had over escaping up and out. But this wasn't exactly helpful as too much meditation left me 'spacey' and, you guessed it, ungrounded. I felt dislocated from others around me. Grounding makes all the difference. Not only do you feel more stable but Mother Earth links with you and recharges your energy through the cord. It is highly important, in learning to manage your symptoms, that you learn how to make a strong, vigorous cord with the Earth. Much of the dizziness and sense of the energy body spinning is due to being ungrounded. Not only is grounding vital to healing, it will reconnect you with your spiritual path and why you are here. Think of it as laying the building block of your path. We will look at healing the chakras in chapter 6.

Once you have learned how to ground with Earth, then you can learn to use this cord to discharge unwanted energies that you pick up, down into the earth for recycling. It has the same principle as a lightning rod discharging electricity to 'earth' in the ground. Discharging is important because you will find that you 'carry' others' energy in your auric field after you have interacted with them. This is likely to cause you to feel heavy and drained. The healing process involves raising your energy field to vigilantly cleanse it of heavy, dense energy.

Discharging unwanted energy
Lie flat in your bed.

Breathe in and sigh out, allowing your body to sink into your bed.

Imagine that you have a lightning rod extending from your tailbone down, down through the bed and deep into the earth beneath you.

Affirm quietly to yourself: *'I release all unwanted energies down into the earth.'* Thank the earth for receiving this energy for recycling.

Visualise the flow of stale energy leaving your body, like water when you turn on the tap. Feel the release as you let it go.

Repeat this twice more, feeling yourself becoming lighter and more peaceful as you let go.

Breathe in and sigh out to expand peace into your energy body which surrounds your physical body.

Lie quietly, savouring the peace and quiet.

Know that this is an important tool in restoring you to full health.

It is vital that you learn how to restore your energy. This will enable you to progress in your healing so that you can have the energy to engage with the other tools in this book. I know this works because I have walked this road to healing and learned these tools along the way.

We cannot avoid interacting with people entirely. That would be the path of loneliness and isolation. Instead, learning about the energy exchange between people which happens in any interaction or conversation gives you the awareness of the need for protection. I found that I needed to minimise dealing with people and to limit the time of each interaction, which I go into further in chapter 6.

So what works to clear your energy field once you're home in your quiet, safe space again?

My favourite cleansing techniques

Wash forehead and hands. My first port of call is to wash my hands in cool water, allowing the water to run over the wrists (there are important energy-discharging points in the inside wrist). Hot water doesn't cleanse energy. After experimenting with various soaps, I found that handmade lavender soap (made with love) is the most uplifting and cleanses best of all. Similarly, I use the soap sparingly and splash cool water in my forehead. I ask the water to cleanse me of others' energy and use my imagination to see heavy energy being washed away: *'I hereby charge this water to cleanse me of others' energy and to clear my energy field.'*

Smudging. A North American smudge stick made from sage is a really powerful tool for cleansing your whole body. Sage is a cooling and cleansing herb which has been used by mankind for thousands of years for its cleansing and uplifting effect. I have also grown sage in my garden and dry the leaves for smudging. Rubbing the fresh leaves between your fingers and breathing in the aroma works well. When I burn it, it tends to stink my house out with smoke, so I light it then step out into my porch to wave my smoke around my body. Use the power of intention to ask the spirit of the sage to cleanse your energy field and raise your vibration. I wave the smoke over my face with my hand and inhale, imagining the smoke cleansing my lungs. Make sure that you wave the smoke front and back, right down to floor level, down the left side and the right. Concentrate the smoke on areas where you feel tense or closed, such as the solar plexus. Continue until you feel clear. Give thanks for the spirit of sage for its powerful effect in transmuting energy.

Lavender or tea-tree oil. Uncapping the bottle and breathing in the oil is a great way of clearing your chakras, similar to wafting a sage smudge stick. A spot of oil on the wrists and brow also is very uplifting. This is useful when it may not be possible to use smoke, for example in a hotel room or on public transport. It is small, portable and unobtrusive for when you are in public.

Shower. Cool water is a highly effective tool for cleansing. I ask the water as I shower to cleanse my energy field by saying, *'I charge this water with cleansing my energy field.'* I imagine it running not only over my body but through it, as if it were hollow, cleaning and clearing inside and out. Cool water is much more effective than hot water; hot water seems to seal the lower energy into the auric field.

Footbath in cold saltwater. I learned this technique from a school of yoga and find it highly effective. Choose a time at the end of the day when you will be undisturbed for 10 minutes. Fill a basin of cold water (enough to cover the ankles) and sprinkle salt into it. Place your feet in the basin. Mentally 'charge' the water with drawing all unwanted energy from your body and imagine it seeping from your feet, turning the water inky in the process. This can be a quiet time for prayer and giving thanks for the day, placing the hands palms up on the thighs. When I am buzzing from several interactions during the day, I can really feel the change in my energy field as it becomes calm in the space of a few minutes. I keep a basin in the bathroom and a jar of sea salt for the purpose. I like this best at the end of the day before bed as it gives me a really restful sleep. On the nights where I am too tired to do this before bed, I find a marked difference as I will have a fitful night's sleep. A big thank-you to those who taught me this!

Try any one or a combination of the above with the intention. Repeating your request three times is a really powerful trans- forming statement in itself. I hope you find them as effective as I do.

Affirmations:
'I choose to be present in this incarnation.'
'I am well grounded.'

Chapter 6

Coping with conversation and public places

You may be aware that certain people are easier to be with than others. Some people exude a calm or compassionate energy which is lovely to be around. Others may harbour resentments or frustrations towards you which make you instinctively withdraw from engaging with them. Some people may be very draining to be with. So why do you feel so bad after seeing him/her? It would be lovely if all interactions left you feeling uplifted, but many conversations are not positive. While your instinct tells you to avoid people whom you find draining, there are occasions when we must interact with other people in the world, especially if you find that you are low in energy and dependent on help. I'd like to explore the energetic exchanges between people and to give you strategies to cope with these. We'll start by examining energy exchanges with strangers.

I've found that people with Chronic Fatigue Syndrome, like me, tend to be too sensitive to the energy around us in our busy consumerist lifestyle. The energies of other people, certain appliances or sounds are just too harsh. I'm sure that this is true for many people as I know that I was aware of it before I became ill, but the extent of the sensitivity needs to be experienced to be properly understood. I'd like to try and give a picture of how this experience feels as well as tips that I discovered which help me to cope.

I used to find it hard, before my collapse, to walk down the pedestrian shopping street in my home town. By the end of the street, I'd be bone-tired. My zest for shopping and all my energy would be gone. I knew I was odd in this respect and wondered how everyone else could enjoy the shopping experience when for me it was a nightmare.

I've come to understand over time that I leaked energy like a sieve. I gave it away to everyone who passed me by: that old lady struggling with a full bag and painful feet got my sympathy; the homeless man with a paper cup sitting dejectedly in a disused doorway; the salesperson with a stressed, harassed look on her face; the dirty children running round the public bench; the angry woman who carried the weight of the world on her prematurely harrowed face, snapping at her children; the lofty man in a business suit distancing himself by looking down his nose; the teenagers jostling me as they push past; hearing harsh language from somewhere behind me; the inadequately dressed baby staring at me with wide, suffering eyes as it was wheeled past. Each interaction took a piece of me and left me in tatters.

I tried not making eye contact because I realised that if I didn't meet anyone's eyes, then it wasn't as bad. Eye contact was the easiest way to 'leak' myself. It made me understand the saying 'eyes are the window on the soul'. I could see right into the heart of everyone I met. I could not only see their pain etched over their faces but feel it inside me, as a tightness, just like physical pain. I tried not catching anyone's eyes but this just didn't feel right. It felt like I didn't care about the suffering I witnessed if I had no response. I felt as callous as a banker or businessman, intent on making money at the expense of others. It felt wrong because I *did* care.

So I started to pray. Maybe I could do nothing much to help the people I saw. Yes, I put money or food in the homeless person's hand. Yes, I smiled at the baby. Yes, I engaged the stressed sales assistant with cheery banter. But it all felt inadequate. A sticking plaster on the overwhelming tide of suffering in one ordinary street, in one ordinary town. With so many similar towns and suffering people all over this planet, what good could I really do? Except pray.

Prayer is a powerful positive act which does make a difference. While I believed my power to be limited, I knew that God's power was limitless. So I prayed for the blessing of God on all the suffering I saw. I asked for alleviation of suffering and peace to all I met. I asked that their spirits be supported through all they had to experience and that they may come to know themselves as spirit having a human journey.

So with these simple blessings I believe that my witnessing of suffering was not in vain. It may seem pointless to a materially minded person but I *felt* different. Blessing others, the blessing comes back to you almost instantly. I would feel better by the end of the street, tired but not totally wiped out. This is because through prayer, we are connecting with the divine, acknowledging our part in the whole. Through our connection, we are suffused with light. Shutting out and walling out others doesn't work because ultimately we are shutting out ourselves. It is through connection with our divine link that we are made whole.

So if you too have witnessed suffering in the faces of others, I invite you to try the simple acts of blessing or prayer spoken silently in your head. Here are a couple of examples, but feel free to change any wording which doesn't appeal to you.

Blessing: *'I bless you that your suffering may be alleviated in the name of love and light.'*
Prayer: *'Divine Father/Mother, I pray that you may send your healing angels to heal this person's suffering and restore peace, in the name of the father, the son and the holy spirit. Amen.'*

The alchemy of prayer is most effective when your prayers are positive affirmations. A prayer asking for more merely reinforces the lack of whatever you are seeking. An example of a positive affirmation would be offering up a prayer of thanks for food or help that you're given, in the present tense, imagining this prayer in a spirit of gratitude for what you have received (even if you haven't received it yet). By the Law of Attraction, we draw that which we believe ourselves to have or be. So choose the wording of your prayer carefully. It is important to positively word your request.

It is interesting that observing others compassionately and being proactive in offering prayers and blessings actually lifts your own spirits. I believe that what you give out you receive, not that I give just to receive, but that the world around us is a mirror of our own internal world. I loved the character Mrs Do-As-You-Would-Be-Done-By in the children's classic *The Water Babies*. This story illustrates in a rich way that what we put out, we get back. A great life lesson for any child to learn early on!

To this day, I treat shopping as a commando raid: in and out as quickly as possible. I can tolerate crowds better now but only for a limited time. In a supermarket, I opt for a basket to do my shopping because I can duck in and out of the trolleys and because it reminds me to only take what I can carry. When my shopping basket is full, it's likely that my personal energy basket will be starting to empty. It is better to leave before I am tired out. I can always come back in a day or two. As I am vegan, I eat a lot of fresh fruit and vegetables. I love it that I am more likely to buy a variety of marked-down food if I pay several short visits to the supermarket in a week and I can save money as well!

Similarly in the town centre, I only visit when I have two or three things that I need. If I only pay for 1 hour's parking, then I seek to complete my moves before the clock strikes midnight and I turn into a pumpkin (or the parking warden fines me). I keep referring to the short list in my hand so that I don't get side-tracked by something I see in a window. Stay on the path, Little Red Riding Hood, lest the wolf gets you and drags all the energy out of you! Sometimes I even talk to myself to keep my mind on the tasks in hand – a sign of sanity, you understand. It helps keep me focused, clear-thinking and I can come away with most of my energy intact. (I try not to let others see, for in this respect, I am still worried what people might think! I have side-stepped people who talked to themselves in the past. But maybe this gives me a wide berth all to myself? Who cares if it works for me?) When you are likely to be overcome with a fuzzy brain, it pays to plan your route through the shops. I write the shop beside the item on my list. I'm continually mindful of my energy reserves and am happy to boycott the trip if any of my warning signs appear (fuzzy mind, face too hot, dizziness etc).

I suggest that you get to know your own warning signs and pay attention to these so that you get out of Dodge before the posse arrives or you might end up in the line of fire! I suggest that you take time to note down your own warning signs of impending energy depletion so that you can seek rest when you feel tired instead of reaching total exhaustion. One friend with M.E. starts to purse her lips and that's a sign to me that she has reached the end of her energy. It's most useful too that your carers know your own 'tells' as well as you. If you ask them, they may be able to enlighten you about a few indicators that you were not aware of.

My observed signs of starting to feel drained:

_____

When I am tiring, others will see that I

_____.

When I am nearing exhaustion, I will feel

_____.

When I'm nearing exhaustion, others will see that I

_____.

Affirmation:
'I am in control of my life.'

Chapter 7

Psychic protection

With the onset of Chronic Fatigue Syndrome came an acute psychic awareness of energetic and unspoken interactions around me. I had only been sporadically aware of this at certain times before. Now I seemed to be on wide-open mode which left me feeling raw, exposed and unprotected. How was I to cope with this new awareness and still retain my sanity? I know that for those who haven't experienced a psychic sensitivity, this talk seems like madness. But I knew deep inside myself that this sensitivity was *right*. That it marked a kind of rite of passage. It was as if I had been living as one of the walking dead before. Now I felt so alive it hurt. I knew, with a deep sense of wisdom, that if only I could learn to cope, then I would live a useful life and be a higher functioning human being than before. So I set about engaging with methods to protect me from the onslaught of psychic waves coming at me and to learn to manage my sensitivity.

So what did I learn? I became aware that prior to the condition, I leaked energy and was like a psychic sponge picking up all manner of lower vibrations and emotions from people. While I had been aware of leaking, I hadn't learned a foolproof method of protection. As I mentioned in the last chapter, being cut off didn't really help. It is my belief that an increasing psychic awareness is one of the markers on the journey to spiritual enlightenment and I decided to welcome this gift. So I dedicated my healing process to accepting my psychic openness and developing protection. I don't think we need to be 100% psychically open, day and night, on this journey. In order to receive rest and to tune into our divine higher self, we can wear a cloak of detachment as protection. Detachment doesn't mean that you are uncaring. On the contrary, detaching from the suffering of this world is essential so that you can tune into your own soul song. Detachment is a difficult lesson to learn, especially if you are used to maintaining a high level of control over your own life and find it hard to act on faith. Spiritual development is essentially the way of wisdom: learning to detach from distractions and to place faith in divine goodness. In a way, your own health issues are a distraction from who you really are. But, at the same time, they are also the most valuable asset you have been given to help you focus on what is real or false about existence.

But you are not alone on this journey. Since you embarked in this incarnation, you have a guardian angel and spirit guides who continually support you in whatever you choose to do in this life. If you ask, they will step forward and offer you their protection. They always guide us with unconditional love and intervene on our behalf if we ask them. They operate within the Law of Free Will and will not violate your free will to make your own choices unless you ask for help. You can ask your guardian angel and guides for protection: *'I ask my guardian angel and spirit guides to offer me protection. Amen.'*

This unconditional help is always open to you with instantaneous results.

There are many methods of protection which you could visualise which would work well. Perhaps you have one that you already use that works for you. Some examples which people have found effective are to imagine you are encased in

- a suit of armour or metal shielding
- a deep-sea diving suit
- a protective cloak or blanket of a colour which feels safe
- an egg of protection that encompasses your entire auric field
- a geometric shape, such as a cube or a pyramid
- a combination of two or more of the above.

A method of protection is most effective when you have generated it for yourself. The following meditation is to travel within your own psyche to find the symbol, or symbols, which feels the most protective for you. When you wear this protection, you will be unaffected by what goes on around you and continue to function with clarity and calm.

It is important that you programme your mode of protection to be permeable to higher vibrations conducive to your healing and spiritual development. It is only unhelpful, lower vibrations which you are blocking out. I usually state that my protection will allow only vibrations from my highest good or that it will only allow fifth-dimensional vibrations and above to pass through.

Meditation to find your own protection symbol

Affirm to yourself that you are going on an internal journey to find your protection symbol. Ask your guardian angel and spirit guides to be with you on your journey.

Breathe in and release out unwanted energy to the trees around.

Attach a grounding cord down to connect with Mother Earth.

Imagine you are in a beautiful garden with flowers of every hue and indescribably beautiful scents. There is a well-tended path which winds uphill. At the top of the hill there is a white temple, its white dome shining in the warm sunshine.

You climb the seven steps up to the temple, feeling lighter with each step.

You step into the entrance of the temple, into a shower of purifying white light. It washes away all residues of tension, filling you with pure white light from your toes to your head.

Inside the high-domed ceiling of the temple, pure light floods in from an unseen source, casting rainbow colours on the floor and walls.

You walk over to stand in front of the altar. Instantly you are clad in your ultimate protection. Gaze down at it and observe it.

Notice how it feels to be in your mode of protection and enjoy it.

When you are ready to leave, keep your armour in place and retrace your path, down the seven steps, becoming more aware of your physical body with each step. Walk down the hill to your starting point in this glorious garden, enjoying how your protection feels around you.

Know that this protection can be donned at any time which brings you back to feeling safe within this place. Breathe in more deeply and open your eyes.

Take time to write about your experiences in your journal.

The effect of stepping up to claim your power and wear your protective symbol can have a huge positive effect. A friend participated in one of my workshops to create her own psychic protection. Afterwards, she related to me that she had always felt intimidated by her family. They habitually chose any family gathering to run her down and belittle her. So before the next family gathering, she asked for angelic help and started to meditate on being contained in her protective egg. She was most surprised that when she got to the door, instead of giving put-down remarks, her brother came to the door and hugged her. He had never done that before. She knew that her work on protecting herself had changed the way that her family perceived her.

Working with the archangels for their protection is very effective. When I was too exhausted to engage in conversation, I would ask Archangel Michael to place me in his protection: *'Archangel Michael, I ask you to cut me free of all cords to everyone and place me in your blue cloak of protection.'*

I would feel immediate relief. In my mind's eye, Archangel Michael stepped forward and severed all cords with his flashing sword and wrapped me lovingly in his blue cloak of protection. This request is powerful with instantaneous results and called on many times a day.

At other times, when I have rested and recovered some energy, I hand over to Archangel Michael and also call on Archangel Chamuel to fill me full of love and light: *'Archangel Michael, I hand over all that is not mine into your care. Archangel Chamuel, please fill me full of Universal Love and Light. Amen.'*

There is an immediate sense of relief in handing over responsibility which helps you to cope with a sense of guilt in letting people down. Your responsibility at this moment is to learn to trust in the divine help and practical support of people around you. The degree that you feel able to let go is the degree to which you can achieve a lightness of being. Imagine Archangel Michael gladly receiving your cares and transmuting them. Imagine Archangel Chamuel stepping forward, smiling, and flooding the space you have cleared inside yourself with Love and Light. Allow yourself to bask in this glorious divine light and gratitude to the divine help you have instantly at hand.

My own particular favourite methods of detachment and protection are, firstly, to call on Archangel Michael to cut me free from ties to others and to place me in his blue cloak of protection. Then I imagine myself inside a pyramid of mirrors which reflects back all that is of a lesser vibration than me. Any stress from others or psychic attack deflects away, leaving me safe inside. I find the square-based pyramid to feel really rigid and strong, with a wide base which connects me well to the earth. Sometimes I continue to add other shapes around this, depending on how I feel, such as a gold orb, a silver sphere and a cube of light. Then my protection feels impregnable to lower vibration intrusion.

Fear is the destroyer of peace and security. You need to build up trust in your divine help and in your own power to create protection. Focus on the light pouring in through your crown and grounding you down into the earth. Mother Earth is delightful to sink down into for protection in the nurturing earth beneath. There have been many sleepless nights when I lay awake in a state of nameless fear. During those times, I felt unable to create a safe haven for myself. My healing journey has been a journey of learning to claim my own power and to trust it. I remember one night I had no sleep at all: I lay awake, continually working with Archangels Michael and Chamuel until the morning. Every time I stopped focusing on my protection, the fear overcame me again. I had instant, if momentary, relief as soon as I asked the archangels again. I mention this because that night was pivotal. Something broke through in me, as if I had passed some sort of initiation or spiritual test. After that, I had faith in generating protection for myself.

So, dear reader, I have faith in you learning to stand in your own power, protected and at peace, no matter the 'storms' which you may face. I invite you to claim your own power and to learn to stand strong.

Affirmation:
'I am strong, safe and secure.'

Chapter 8

Sensitivity to sound and ELF (extremely low frequencies of electromagnetic energy)

It is difficult to say which came first: *the chicken or the egg?* The sensory sensitivities or the fatigue? Even as a child, I realise that I heard sound differently to most people. The stereotypical 'chalk on a blackboard' screech wasn't offensive to me, although it had everyone else's teeth on edge. No, for me that was well within the normal sound range and quite easy to cope with. I wondered why everyone else found that alarming.

My hearing was much more acute than that. I could hear very high-pitched sounds which others could not hear, such as the squeaks of bats flying overhead. Sometimes I was dismissed as making it up as a child. Although, why a child would make up something like that escapes me!

I remember driving to university in my mum's old car and the problematic days when it rained. The windscreen wipers had a high-pitched squeal that the other students in the car couldn't hear but which gave me a sick migraine. Also, the sibilant 'sss' sound of certain higher-pitched female voices or the low vibratory hum through the wall of a tumbler drier or the vacuum cleaner next door have the ability to unhinge me.

Subsonic or high-pitched frequencies are very difficult to shut out and insistent in my head. They put my teeth on edge and make it hard to focus on anything else. Sometimes certain sounds even make me feel nauseous. I can walk into a room and be disturbed by appliances on standby 'singing' in a high-pitched frequency. TVs, DVD players, some light bulbs, games consoles and even multi-point plug extensions all create a singing noise when on standby which disturbs my brain frequency. I sometimes find it hard to link my thoughts and remain focused because the sound interferes with my brain waves. I can be stopped dead in my tracks by an insistent singing from plugs and chargers which commands my attention.

I have watched a sheepdog suddenly prick up its ears and turn to look when my grandfather blew the dog whistle, a sound which, bearing in mind my auditory sensitivity, was inaudible to me. I don't hear the sound emanating from a household rodent deterrent either, although I get the feeling that something is playing at the edges of my internal vision, just beyond my hearing, as if there is an associated colour or smell, rather than hearing. It's hard to describe. It makes me wonder if others with so-called normal hearing are also disrupted by these high-pitched electronic sounds, even if they don't hear them? If that is the case, I am concerned about the sheer mass of electronic devices that are commonly plugged in behind a multi-media console. Perhaps another indicator of our mass dumbing down is that we can't perceive the sound emanations. Neither do we care as we become used to more and more wired and wireless appliances which, reason tells me, must have an effect on the human brain. I am deeply concerned about Wi-Fi hubs being harmful to our bodies. I pity the children who are, day in, day out, seated within 10 feet of a Wi-Fi hub in schools. What effect will that radiation have on the young developing brain? Or the effect of the constant interference to their energy bodies? Sometimes we don't need to wait for science to do research; with inner wisdom and inner sight, we just *know* that something is wrong. I gave up using a microwave oven many years ago for that very reason. I just knew that, at a cellular level, each cell is made of photons or light at its centre so zapping food by breaking down cells from the inside out was just wrong. Science was later to discover that microwave ovens radiate microwaves within 20 feet while food is cooking and the food will continue to 'cook', radiating these same microwaves for a few minutes after removal from the oven. Using a microwave oven puts the user in danger of cooking their own organs in the process and anyone else who comes close!

The electromagnetic field and low hum emanating from low ceilings with fluorescent strip lighting overhead can be problematic. It is well known that a flickering strip light can trigger migraines and epileptic fits in those with a predisposition towards those conditions. But even a functioning strip light seems to disrupt my thinking, especially if the ceiling is low. I recall one particular room where I used to meet other teachers to collaborate on new initiatives but where I was rendered useless because my brainwaves felt scrambled. In comparison with many other meeting rooms, there was something noticeably detrimental about that one. It had a low ceiling with a strip light a few feet above my head. There is a modern architectural trend to reduce room dimensions of all new builds of public buildings in an effort to cut costs. Restricted room size places a stress on us as humans, being cramped in on top of each other like rats in a cage. It's not surprising when we can feel tense and irritable. Voyeuristic TV shows, like *Big Brother*, illustrate my point nicely. As a person sensitive to changes in electromagnetic energy and to close proximity of others' energy fields, I can fully appreciate the term 'a sick building'.

There is a causal link between low, subsonic ELF and M.E./CFS (see bibliography). A friend very effectively demonstrated the ELM (electromagnetic) field of household appliances to me, using the aerial of an old transistor radio. It crackled with static as he walked within a few feet of electric light bulbs and ticked like a Geiger counter within 2 feet of a wireless tablet. Even electric plug points and the wires within the walls leak ELM radiation and were picked up by this machine. This wonderfully simple demonstration is an easy way for you to measure the ELM fields around your home and is something which you can try yourself. I was at last able to understand why I can only sleep well at one side of my bedroom – the side away from the electric plug sockets and the hidden cables within the plasterboard wall.

It makes you re-evaluate how much we are affected by noise. Our modern lives, filled with appliances which emit microwaves and radiation, are also bombarding us with sound, both audible and that beyond our hearing range. I am highly aware of the value of silence around me. It is like a balm. Peace and restoration for my soul. I have never understood those people who can listen to music and read or study at the same time. Music playing in the background disrupts my ability to maintain focus on a train of thought or to recall another song while one is playing. I enjoy a big silence around me to spread into. That's what engenders the best environment for me. I am not suggesting that you are the same, but I would like you to take time to think about the probable effect of sound in your environment.

Practical methods to reduce exposure to sound and electromagnetic fields in your home

1. Limit use of a modem and internet to 10 minutes a day. Switch off the modem when not in use.
2. Limit use of TV, computer screens and mobile or wireless phones which emit electromagnetic waves. Be conscious that wireless appliances receive and emit harmful waves which also pass through you.
3. Do not microwave food. Use a little water in the bottom of a pan to re-heat food, stirring constantly. Plates placed on top of the pan will heat nicely in the steam. Just wipe the plates dry before serving up.
4. Remove TV and all electrical appliances from your bedroom. Develop a quiet haven which is not contaminated by the broadcasts, conversations or emotional onslaught of those with a less sensitive nature in this world.
5. Wherever possible, site your bed away from electrical plug sockets and electrical cables.

6. Soundproof the walls of your quiet space if necessary. I stapled two layers of laminate floor underlay onto the adjoining wall backing onto my neighbour. As a decoration, I covered this with fabric in a calming colour as a feature wall. As a bonus, using a wall stapler is quicker and less effort than painting a wall.

7. When seeking to move house, consider the proximity of the nearest electrical substation or pylon. If you currently live near these, it may be wise to explore relocation.

Just as a beautiful chord on a piano or a beautiful composition has the ability to transfix and bring us to a state of rapture, so has a discordant frequency the ability to disrupt brain frequencies. It sends alarm bells ringing through me to hear about HAARP research into subsonic sound waves being used to alter the weather or being used as a weapon to affect normal human brain functioning.

Sound has the capability to heal or break us. In his wisdom, Edgar Cayce stated that 'sound is the medicine of the future'. That is how important sound is to us. You may be interested to read about *cymatics* which is a study of patterns which appear in sand when subjected to sound-wave vibration on a metal plate. The sand forms the most beautiful regular patterns. Hans Jenny's experiments with cymatics demonstrate how ancient Hebrew and Sanskrit languages create regular patterns when their vibration is played through sand on a metal plate. Order from chaos. Imagine the effect of various frequencies on our molecules? All possibilities are open to us as humans to use the power of our will to create harmony or hell. I know which one I want for us all!

As a learning support teacher, I often worked with children who had sensitivity to certain sound frequencies as I did and suffered stress from the inability to filter out the constant noise of a classroom. Many children find it hard to block extraneous noise, especially those who are on the autistic spectrum. Being sensitive myself, I taught them desensitisation life skills in a quiet location, outside the problematic environment. Children have an amazing capacity to learn quickly and they responded very well to learning meditation. I taught them the coping strategy that I'm about to teach you. It is a meditation to instil calm, thereby reducing the hyper-alert state. It aims to refocus attention inward, develop the sense of inner sight by visualising the space you occupy, and create environmental protection around yourself. I believe that this is a life skill which we would all benefit from learning while we are children, as a coping strategy for life.

Meditation to focus on detracting attention and refocusing
Sit comfortably and gently close your eyes.

Imagine breathing in white light through the crown of your head.

Allow that white light to flow through your body and out through your tailbone, creating a root which links deep down into the centre of the earth.

Focus for a moment on white light to flow through your crown and out into the earth.

Feel the energetic response of light flow back up from the heart of the earth herself.

Sit quietly savouring the light pouring into you from above and below. You sit in a column of white light, suspended between heaven and earth.

Imagine you are now sitting in a pyramid of mirrors. The mirrors reflect back to the world all that doesn't resonate with you, including sounds and lower vibrations. Only the highest and purest energy can enter this safe, healing space inside the pyramid.

Feel and appreciate the calm within your pyramid. It is a

strong protection around you.

Sit for as long as you wish. Keep this structure in place when you return to the outside world. With practice, it can be visualised very quickly to create immediate relief from sounds and other intrusions.

Sound can be created consciously to raise your light quotient and resilience. Sound is the essential component building block of the universe. In the Bible, John 1 states: 'In the beginning was the Word, and the Word was with God, and the Word was God.' In yogic traditions, 'Om' is said to be the sound at the centre of creation. Sound is the resonation which created and holds the structure of the universe intact. At the centre of all things, there is sound.

Listening deeply to the sound within you with single-pointed focus is a calming and centring practice which can lead to enlightenment.

There is a story about a man who was seeking enlightenment:

A man once went to visit a wise guru to find the path to enlightenment. He asked the guru what he should do to reach enlightenment. The guru told him to sit and empty himself and to listen deeply, so deeply that he heard a sound like a thousand tiny bells. So, diligently, the man sat every day from sunrise until sunset, listening. He could hear all the sounds of nature around him and the sounds of his body within him. At times his attention wandered but still he sat expectantly waiting. Hundreds of day passed and still the man didn't hear a sound like a thousand tiny bells. He learned about the peace of just listening. He learned that silence isn't silent. That even in the absence of external sound, there is sound. But still he didn't hear a thousand tiny bells. Day after day he sat until he reached the point when he was about to give up and go home, so finally he decided to sit one more day. Just as the sun was going down and he gave up trying, he heard it: a musical tinkling sound that seemed to come from above, beneath and inside him, a sound exactly like thousands of tiny bells. And then he knew that connection with all that is through sound at the heart of creation.

I like this story. It reminds me, when things are exhausting and I am laid up resting, that all I need do is listen. Your body may be tired and in need of total rest, but actively listening is achievable. Beyond the chatter of your own internal voice and the play of images in the flow of your thoughts, behind all that, you can listen to your own unique sound within the universe: the song of your soul.

Deep inner listening to the sound of your soul song
Choose a time when you will be uninterrupted.

Close your eyes and withdraw into your safe, quiet space.

Connect your grounding cord into the earth and up to your highest self through your crown chakra. Create a golden cloak of protection around yourself, with a hood covering your head.

Listen to the sounds around you. Allow all these sounds to filter through without attaching any thought to them. You may find your mind imagining the scene you can hear outside but gently disengage from this thought train. Tell yourself that these sounds are irrelevant.

Gradually allow your listening to turn inward, into your body. What can you hear inside your body? You may hear blood in your ears, the beat of your heart or your breathing.

Then disengage from the sounds of the body. Train yourself to listen deeper and beyond the physical body. What is the sound behind and beyond? It will be a sweet, constant note, which is your resonating soul song. You will know it because it makes you feel well and happy.

Imagine your soul song becoming stronger. Allow it to

resonate through your aura. Imagine it glowing more brightly.

Bring that resonation through to your physical body, helping your body to remember healthy and healing vibrations. Imagine your physical body glowing more brightly. Bask in the healing song of your soul.

Listening to your soul song restores and heals. It brings you to a state of resonance with your soul purpose in this incarnation. It can be helpful to sing or intone your note aloud.

Sound has a huge impact on our lives, some of which you may be conscious of. In your journal, make a list of all the instances where sound has impacted positively on you and another list where sound has been detrimental to your health. It may be that certain frequencies or situations deliver you to a state of calm.

Reflect on situations where you 'leak energy' very quickly, such as in a supermarket, an electrical store or a doctor's surgery.

Have you got sensitivity to the radiation from the electrical appliances around you?

Are there places where you seem less affected?

How can you limit your exposure to sound or ELM?

Plan one or two ways where you might bring changes in your life to create a more harmonious space for your recovery.

Affirmation:
'I create peace and harmony around me.'

Life, I feel too extremely,
The pulse of the world too harsh:
In sordid sagas and sought-after news,
the beat of the music too loud.
I have no draw,
to be so raw,
to bite at the knuckles at which I gnaw.
Where is the peace in a bitter-sweet world?
For I feel like a stranger in a strange land,
too finely tuned for the ragged pitch and pace.
I would rest and be still if I find such a place:
A haven for this hapless warrior,
licking world-afflicted wounds.
So ever more inward I curl from outward clamour,
inwardly winding on a road traversed by pilgrims,
succour at the lotus heart of myself,
nurture and nestle, recharge and strength,
awake refreshed,
to walk placidly once more...

Chapter 9

Pleasing other people

Trying to please other people has been a constant theme in my life. As far back as I look, I found it hard to say no. So small a word. So difficult to say because I wanted to be liked. Maybe if I performed well, gave of myself, my time, my money, then I'd be liked. Surely?

It is fitting that pleasing other people, often when it goes against what's best for you, appealed to a self-sacrificing Christian ethic. It seemed a plausible reason to my girlish mind. But the underlying truth was I was afraid to say no. That the person concerned would just walk away and reject me...

And I bring myself back to being miserable, shy and feeling alien from everyone in my first few years at school. I had no friends. I envied the other girls their easy manner with each other, while I was contorted in on myself with self-consciousness. I thought I had to be someone else, someone interesting, someone fun. It took me years to realise that all I ever needed was to be myself, truly myself.

So, in the playground I was in a daily nightmare scenario of feeling like I stood out like a sore thumb, like an alien in a human world where I didn't know the rules of interaction. In an attempt to avoid feeling so contorted and awful, and being incredibly skinny, I found I could squeeze behind the drainpipe against the red sandstone building and be invisible. Nobody bothered me here. I would spend most of my playtime hidden in the hope that no one would find me. Here I would further crawl inside the shell of myself where I found a well of dejectedness so deep that it frightened me. The abyss had no end. No matter how I fell like Alice into this rabbit hole, I never reached the bottom. I could shout and wail inside myself but the sound disappeared into nothingness. Only the bell ringing to signal return to the safe, structured environment of the classroom drew me forth again from this internal world. In the classroom, I knew the rules. All I had to do was perform. That was easy.

Everything changed when my younger sister came to school when I was 7. I watched her make friends and play at ease with everyone. That should have helped me take a cue from her, but instead I avoided my own classmates and clung to her and her circle of friends during the dreaded playtimes. She was like my life raft on an uncharted and turbulent sea. With her, I felt safe because she knew me, the real quiet me, better than anyone. I didn't need to prove myself to her and she liked me as her older sister just as I was. But with everyone else, I tried to be someone other than me because I felt I wasn't good enough as myself.

I wonder if everyone with Chronic Fatigue Syndrome or M.E. just tries too hard to please? I recognise a common need for approval. We are too terribly concerned with what others might think. This could be a generality for us as humans. And whom does it serve to be so self-sacrificing? So worried that you'll be judged as inadequate? If it doesn't serve yourself, then question the reason why you *are* doing it. Be prepared to acknowledge motives that don't fit with the nice, wholesome view that you have of yourself. And don't be too hard on yourself either if you find a petty, small, childish response – this is all part of the growth, or rather re-growth of yourself into a blossoming, whole human being. The first step is to truthfully acknowledge the undercurrent and the real truth of motivation.

For instance, and here is one of my unwholesome truths, I only realised once I was too ill, too drained, that in seeking to avoid unfavourable responses, such as anger, in others, I have been reaching out in the ethers to 'salve' others. As far back as I can remember I have been really sensitive to the change in the emotional atmosphere in a room, particularly as regards my mother. Without really understanding what I was doing, I have been reaching out to smooth down that person's auric field, as if smoothing ruffled feathers down. I was always disturbed by, even afraid of, the anger response in others because emotional outbursts would jar on me. I would be afraid that I would not be liked if others found me wanting and were angry with me. I found that if I reached out with my energy field, I could defuse anger reactions and bring others to a state of calm.

When I collapsed with Chronic Fatigue Syndrome, if I attempted to reach out energetically to perform my habitual, unconscious smoothing, I found I had no energy to do so. It pulled me up short and made me realise just how much I had sought to control others in the past from a motivation of fear that I would fall out of favour with them. This was unwholesome as the primary motives were for selfish reasons. It came to me, only when I was unable to do so, that this was wrong because I was interfering with how others wished to conduct themselves. I now believe that a healthier approach is to detach and allow them to express themselves as they wish. Just as I am at liberty to express myself freely, so too should others be. It is not my responsibility to 'dampen' down the emotional response in others. What would be right would be to live and let live: detach, protect myself and bless others – a much more healthy approach. You may or may not agree that this was wrong, but ultimately, on this very personal journey in this vessel that we call a human body, we must all come to terms with conducting ourselves from the highest possible motive that we can. This is just one example of how my illness has served me by showing me the truth of myself. If I had not been caught short by my illness, I would have continued to interfere by smoothing down others. It was wrong because I did it for reasons of personal gain.

I have come to realise that there is a clear pattern leading up to my outbreak of Chronic Fatigue Syndrome that, in trying to please and impress others, I sacrificed myself.

Dealing with strangers is sometimes easier than conversations with family and friends, especially those relationships you find taxing. So what is energetically happening in those interactions which result in you feeling strained or drained? Prior to having Chronic Fatigue Syndrome, I could sense the energetic interaction between myself and another but I didn't understand it then. It was only when I was lying there, wide open to all energies and relying heavily on my family support, that my understanding and awareness of the invisible interplay of energy developed. Sometimes I 'see/feel' the streamers of light stretching from one person to another. I am aware when someone tries to 'take' my energy or push me, even when the conversation is hiding this exchange. Sometimes I glimpse an energy tentacle sneaking in or snaking in to 'suck' some of my energy like a psychic vampire. Other times, I become aware of this intrusion only when I feel stressed, and instinctively fold my arms in an unconscious attempt to shield my solar plexus.

I would like to talk to you about energy body exchanges between you and other people. I will teach you how to develop an awareness of what is happening that may be hidden from the outward exchange and how to deal with it.

All energy exchanges can be either positive or negative. Positive interactions nourish us and make us feel happy. Negative interactions cause us damage and make us feel ill. People's auras oscillate at different vibratory rates. When someone has a strong field with a higher energy around them, they raise the vibratory rate of those they come in contact with. When someone has a strong field but a lower vibratory rate, they lower the field of others around them. When two or more people come in tune with each other, their energy bodies vibrate sympathetically. You will know when you are in harmony with someone when you find conversation easy and there is no resistance, as if you are both 'speaking the same language'. Another sign that you are coming into synchronicity is when you unconsciously mirror each other's gestures.

However, there are times when conversing with people or even being in their presence is not harmonious. Even if there is an outward display of friendliness, you can feel as if you are being attacked. I would like to acquaint you with the unspoken energy exchanges of people so that this helps you to respond positively, in a healing manner, to people around you. You will be able to recognise when negative interactions are taking place and how to protect yourself when you feel pushed, pulled, brow beaten, or your energy sucked away.

There are five main types of negative energy interactions:

1. Sucking: The person doing this will send out cords from their solar plexus to 'suck' from your solar plexus. They will attempt to hook on and drain you. Be aware that this is not your imagination. They will also attempt to hold your eye contact and drain your energy through your eyes. Try not to give them eye contact and don't sit or stand facing them. Instead, imagine you have a shield over your solar plexus chakra such as a metal belt.

2. Looming: The person doing this will pull up their aura out of their body, tower over you and push at you. You will know it is happening because you feel under threat as if you are being 'brow beaten'. You can deal with this person by grounding down into the earth and having strong roots. Remember, they can't hurt you if you keep your main awareness in your strong connection to the earth. Imagine that you have your impenetrable barrier around you so that you remain unaffected by their auric pushing. Wait quietly for them to finish speaking before speaking yourself.

3. Pushing away and taking: The person doing this both demands and resists at the same time. They will try to lead you into heavy conversation while pushing you out and rejecting all your suggestions. This type of energy interaction can be very tiring. It is best not to stand or sit close to this person or to face them as they will attempt to send barbed cords into your solar plexus and hook onto your energy. Place your hands over your solar plexus and imagine your impenetrable barrier around you.

4. The empty shell: The person doing this withdraws their energy slightly out of their physical body in order to feel safe. You will know when someone is doing this because their eyes glaze over and it's as if there is no one home. The more you try to 'reach' this person energetically, the more withdrawn they will become. Instead, be aware of any pushing that you are doing and pull your energy back into your own aura. Try to sit or stand side by side and bring yourself to a state of calm inside. Imagine you are standing on green grass under some trees with roots grounding down into the earth.

5. The plastic person: This person can seem removed from the conversation and just be on automatic. Everything they do can seem just too perfect, which can make you feel flawed. However, perhaps you were once someone who tried just too hard. Try to feel compassion for this person who doesn't yet know, as you do, that outward appearances and trying to be perfect have their toll. Reaffirm, silently, that you are perfect just as you are.

I believe it is helpful to have a deeper understanding of the subtle energy interactions involved in dealing with the people around you. It is not your imagination that certain people in your life, while seeming to be understanding or helpful, can in fact be taking your energy. I think it is empowering for you to know that this can happen and to help you recognise when this is occurring. This will give you the chance to prepare your protection in advance of a meeting. With practice, you can 'snap on' your mode of protection with one thought. In the world of thought, creation is instant. As you think, so it is.

Take time to reflect in your journal about those people who leave you feeling drained. Have you been aware of a secret interaction that maybe you couldn't quite place before? Reflect on which character type they are likely to be and why.

Practise donning your protection so that you can achieve it at a moment's notice.

Protection should become second nature. Until you are programmed to remember your protection, it can be helpful to draw yourself inside your protection, smiling and safe. The visual image will help you to remember.

Your etheric body is a shining double of your physical body. Your issues are like lots of etheric 'buttons' just asking to be pressed. While not visible to the physical eye, these 'issue buttons' will unconsciously either draw or repel others. Think about situations where you, against your will, found yourself doing or saying something totally uncharacteristic. Have you ever wondered why you did that? Said something that you didn't mean to say but to which the other responded in a way which suddenly affirmed to you that it was something meaningful to them? You are likely to be responding to their 'buttons' without realising it. You were unconsciously acting to fulfil their emotional need. This need can direct you to respond with either a positive reaction or a negative reaction.

So take a look at your own emotional buttons. It is pointless and just plain tiring to habitually react in the same old way. If you change your auto-response to emotional triggers, then your thoughts will also change.

Choose one reaction at a time and make it the release of the week.

Once, when I was involved with a local eco-project, one of my roles was to manage a community garden. The lesson I learned from this was that not everyone can be your friend. I found I had a flair for leading and motivating participants by assigning the volunteers' tasks suitable to their level of ability and harnessing their particular talents. However, a manager is required to be unpopular at times for the good of the community group and to fulfil the aim of the project. If someone breaks the democratically agreed rules, a manager can't manage without asserting authority by having words with the member whose behaviour is at odds with the project. One is required to be potentially unpopular. A serious challenge to someone who has a need to be liked. Do I 'smooth' my way through the period of dissent (manipulating from fear of disagreement)? Do I ignore it and hope it'll rectify itself (choosing inaction from fear of conflict)? Or do I have the courage to speak to the person face to face (overcoming the fear of not being liked or being unpopular)?

This work with the community group served me as a lesson to place a greater good above my need to please. So I have learned that I must speak my truth, despite the fear of not being liked. I learned that the need to appear capable at all costs and to be approved of doesn't always serve me. I learned that me acting in a self-sacrificing way to appease others doesn't serve me either.

So while I was flat on my back, I became hyper-aware of the energy exchanges between people and towards me. But I also began to be aware of instinctive ways that I used to relate to them. I began to wonder: were my habitual energy interactions with others healthy? When I realised that I smoothed people down, I wondered what else I did in an attempt to control. Did I 'steal' others' energy? It can be a shock when you realise that your squeaky clean image of yourself isn't the whole truth.

I would suggest that you take a few moments here to examine your true motivations in reaction to situations you are facing. Motivations are often multifaceted. You may have 50% of your reaction stemming from guilt, 40% from fear and 10% from spite because that person has previously hurt you. We often have a front-line motivation which we are willing to share with others as it shows us in a favourable light, but be prepared to look behind that façade. Are you a 'poor me' or a bully? It's time to be honest with yourself. No one else to impress here. It's like giving yourself a spring clean: clear out the old to bring in the new. Do you really want to retain the old clutter? Stale old motivations and habitual patterns? I for one found this process of internal clearing very cathartic!

Look through the list of negative interaction types, this time in relation to your own behaviours. Do you withdraw? Create walls? Push at others? Pull at them? Do you have a secret agenda that you don't speak openly about? Do you place barbs or hooks in someone? Write your thoughts in your journal.

Be objective but don't stand in judgement of yourself.

Acknowledge which particular energy interaction you habitually use.

Be aware of where in the body you feel it from.

Next, close your eyes and visualise if you have cords attached to anyone and who they are. You will know who because the picture of a person's face or a name will come into your head immediately. It could be someone you have a close relationship to or it could be someone surprising, such as a woman you spoke to in the car park or an old friend from school. Some cords are from past lives. Negative cords look ugly in dark, muddy colours like a coiled rope, umbilical cord or an eel. Positive cords are light and don't feel heavy or ugly. In the first instance, you would be concerned with cutting the negative cords as these only take your life force away. Positive cords are involved in giving you energy as well as taking and these were attached with love. Ultimately, any cord is an attachment which means that you are not independently standing in your own power so you may wish to tackle positive cords at some point in the future, but I would advise that you work to remove all negative cords as these will be detrimental to your health. Sometimes the sender of a cord attachment will be subtly aware when you have cut the cord and you may have the impression that they are not pleased to have your power source denied to them.

These cords can be from any chakra. The following exercise should be done several times over the first week, tackling a different chakra each time. You should repeat the exercise regularly as cord attachments can happen again many times after the initial clearing.

Decording exercise

Sit in meditation, ground into the earth and place your protection around you.

Call on your angel and guides to be present to guide and protect you.

View one chakra. Ask to be shown negative cords from that chakra. You will have a mental image of the cords.

Choose one cord at a time. Ask to be shown who it belongs to. You may see an event from your past played out as a movie or a snapshot image.

Call on Archangel Michael to cut the cords to that person. See the cord snapping back to the recipient.

Repeat for each cord attached to that chakra.

Ask your guides and angels to cleanse and heal the chakra with pure white light. Imagine placing a protective shield over it.

Thank your guides, angels and Archangel Michael and ask for their continued protection.

Drink plenty of water to flush your system.

Have a cool shower or bath. Wash the chakra with salt to cleanse, and rinse with fresh water.

Affirmation:
'I see and understand my interactions with crystal-clear clarity.'

Chapter 10

Coping with others' mixed reactions

My unreliability has been difficult for my friends and family to accept, especially when there is an expectation of you. Although I've taken to warning others before I go out that I will probably only manage to wait an hour or two before I have to leave, this isn't always well received. The need to leave can arise very suddenly, like a panic which is caused by overstimulation, an assault on my nervous system and energy leakage from my precious accumulated store, built up over several days of rest.

On one occasion, I went to a local peace conference with friends. I've learned that it is better for me to arrive on my own so that I'm not exposed to too much stimulation or conversation on the journey there but also so that I can leave at short notice as the urge to leave usually comes suddenly, like an assault wave: 'I've had enough!' is spoken insistently in my head. My friends were pleased to see me arrive. Unfortunately, they had seated themselves in the middle of the second front row. I like to sit at the edge, further back so that I can leave easily and discreetly. Not quite happy with the seating arrangement, I sat beside my friends but then some family members arrived and blocked my exit from that row. They all wanted to engage me in conversation before the conference started, in sympathetic concern about my health and genuine pleasure in seeing me out. So even before the event, I was feeling hemmed in and engaging in too much conversation, in close body proximity (which leaves me more susceptible to the harmonic convergence of their energy fields). Sometimes it's easier to sit with strangers. I can shut off from them, preserve and protect my energy better.

So, then the conference started. It was a really inspiring and interesting presentation of uplifting humanitarianism in action across the planet. However, as soon as the speakers started, I was aware of the focus of attention from the audience behind me, moving *through* my energy field. I felt raw and exposed. It was too much. I steeled myself to sit tight until the speakers were over (interesting word choice, for if I was truly steel-armoured, then perhaps I'd be able to cope! The techniques of protection are less effective in a state of anxiety). It was a fight within myself not to get up and leave, thereby disturbing the whole row and drawing the attention of everyone in the hall. Polite training of a well brought-up girl overrode my need to leave. I managed to wait for about an hour, no more, until a change of speakers gave me a moment when I could leave. Unfortunately, one of my friends took offence when I wanted to leave. She was feeling rejected because of the number of previous occasions when I'd left her sitting. She is one of many people unable to comprehend how Chronic Fatigue and being oversensitive feels. I was accused of 'playing the Fatigue Card' once too often and trying to control everyone with my illness.

I'm only bringing this up as an example of the attitudes which you may experience as a reaction to your illness. 'You were always OK before, so why aren't you OK now?'

Something you have to deal with time and time again with Chronic Fatigue Syndrome is the disbelief of others that there's anything wrong with you. It's not like there are many visible signs of dis-ease, and others may doubt your condition, observing you from their own position of strength and good health, saying things like 'Just try a bit harder' or 'If you believe you're weak, you're weak – it's all in the mind'. And even things like 'I don't believe you're ill, you're just attention seeking'. These are all reactions which I have received.

And to be truthful, I would have made similar judgements prior to my illness. It's amazing how judgemental and 'pass-remarkable' we can be when we're looking from the outside in. I remember one colleague at work with M.E. who would struggle to fulfil the daily requirements and strains of being a primary teacher. At the time I thought, from my elevated stance of good health, that she had a poor attitude and that she was acting like a victim. There was a particular expression on her face which has stuck in my mind, as if the world had an offensive smell. She wrung her hands in an ingratiating manner which irritated me. Why? Her gestures were those of a victim, expecting a beating, like a cowering cur. It is a shameful human admission but one feels the tendency to kick something when it's cringing in expectation of a kick, as if you almost want to fulfil their obvious expectation. Of course, I'm not the kind of person who would lash out, but still I was aware of repressing the reflex impulse. Or, at the very least, shunning her illness like a contagion which might be catching. We have a natural disgust of ill-health as a base instinct for self-preservation.

My judgement was that she'd assigned her own sentence due to a negative attitude to the world. It was her sour attitude which caused others to shy away from her in dislike. She was 'othered' for me. I judged that she didn't make an effort to cope like I did. But how the mighty will fall! What a shock to find out that it could happen to me!

Which got me to thinking, why had I not felt sympathy for someone who obviously was struggling more than I was? She was finding ways of managing and literally 'holding herself together' through wringing her hands. Instead of sharing burdens and stresses like you do with other colleagues and human beings, a weak one in the group is shunned.

It's only when you walk a mile in another man's shoes that you realise that this perspective is the flawed one. Unconsciously, when you're too sensitive to the conversations, to the energy field clashes with others, you do tend to put up barriers as an instinctive self-protection. Compassion, if not understanding, is what you need from others, not condemnation. So little understood, so little found. Compassion then is the big lesson. I am now of the belief that it is only through experiencing a condition first hand that we can truly understand. In that moment, there is an epiphany of understanding, as if the veil which separates us were being lifted. Suddenly you can see through their eyes, feel as they/you feel for the first time and realise that there is no separation. That this body which I inhabit is not a real barrier when we enter the world of feelings. In 'feeling' we can 'know' how the other is on the inside and be conscious of the fact that it is no different from ourselves.

Compassion works both ways. We can have compassion towards perceived weakness and towards those who perceive themselves as strong. I have been able to adjust my perception in regards to one whom I judged as weaker and those whom I saw as stronger. Compassion towards perceived differences of any kind has been a great lesson.

I also learned to be compassionate towards myself struggling with feelings of guilt in letting others down. Time and time again, my family and friends have been put out or put off by me when I felt overwhelmed or afraid that the situation would be too much for me. I can understand that my unreliability would be a pain in the ass. Fluctuations in how I feel are, by their very nature, unpredictable. If I rested up, that gave me strength to deal with a forthcoming event: little stress or other commitments for a few days prior gave me a 'store' of quiet strength which might see me through. I used to feel almost panicky, no, downright panic and backed into a corner when suddenly another agenda was imposed on me. This wasn't OCD. Or a control freak freaking out. I didn't have this reaction prior to the diagnosis of CFS. This panic was based on learned evidence to me that 3 or 5 days of rest helped me to do some of the things I wanted to do, like my birthday party. I'm usually exhausted for a few days after events like this but the exhaustion can be much more severe if I don't have the prior rest to build up a store of energy.

This is called 'pacing yourself'. I learned about this when I attended the Graduated Exercise Therapy (GET) offered by physiotherapy. It's all about learning what works for you so that you can pace yourself without depleting your body's energy. I learned so much from this approach and from just trial and error, that I can do all that I want to (within reason!). I think it's worth noting here that my horizons have narrowed somewhat since my diagnosis; if I can't do everything, then at least now I'm realistic in my expectations of my capabilities.

When you have established your warning flags (chapter 6) you can put this into action in those moments you realise that you are beginning to tire. At that time, what would be most healing would be to withdraw from energetic connection and to limit the time you spend in conversation. This can be awkward when well-meaning family and friends try to help you. It serves you best to be honest and voice what is best for your healing progress. Even if this will vary from day to day, or even hour to hour. It will serve you best to speak up and act in a way which is healing and restorative for you.

However, you will have to face the anger and disappointment of those left holding the fort on your rest period, on the days when you 'play the CFS card', apologise and have to bow out graciously. This isn't always well received. In fact, some reactions can be pretty extreme. One time, when I was scheduled to babysit my grandchildren, I got myself into an awful state, feeling overwhelmed by how much energy it would take out of me while I recognised the need to rest in order to prepare for a forthcoming trip away with friends, which I knew would be taxing enough on its own. I got myself into a state of alarm, caught between what I knew was best for me and the support my daughter needed. I felt upset that I was a constant letdown for her. I'm really grateful for the compassion she has shown me over all of this. But others have not been so understanding, saying things like 'What's actually wrong with you anyway? Where's your treatment? What's your medication? I don't believe there's anything wrong with you – just try harder!' That's when holding a space of compassion is the only healing response for you and towards them. How little do they know. Hindsight is a great leveller. My younger self did not understand what it feels like so I can be compassionate to those who do not understand me. All part of the universal Law of Reflection.

Others' disbelief can be hard to cope with. But still, stick to your guns. Becoming well is about doing what's best for you. Not what's best for everyone else. You've tried that and that's what burned you out in the first place. I invite you to give yourself permission to act in the way which best suits your health, as no one really understands how it feels for you. If it's real for you, then it is real.

My advice is to limit the number of occasions that you go out and to choose wisely where you sit. In a restaurant, I find that a large, open space is better than being crushed in close proximity with other diners. Also, use your intuitions, before you sit, to ascertain which table 'feels right'. A Yes or No response in your abdomen is your guide. I trust and listen to it now. I also speak up quickly to the group, before they all sit, and say where *feels* best for me.

In a cinema, I choose to sit near the back, behind the emotional reaction of others to the film, as we tend to throw our emotions out the front of our bodies. It also helps to wait a week or two after the premiere, as the cinema is likely to be less busy.

In a theatre I am careful, for the same reasons, not to sit too near to the front (I compromise here because my mother loves the front row!). But the content of the play or performance is my main consideration. If the narrative is likely to be too harrowing or the actors are too good at portraying emotion, I feel the onslaught in the stalls; then I'm better off not agreeing to go. Again, using your intuition to 'feel' ahead how the play is likely to be at the buying-of-the-tickets stage is wise. It's all a bit of a compromise really. It is difficult because you have fears of slipping back into a bedridden state, unable to do much for yourself, but also you have the wishes of others to take into consideration.

Before entering any public building where there is likely to be many 'sick', anxious or drunk people, my advice is to prepare before you go. Visualise your protection. Put your auric field in closer to yourself and place a metal shield in front of your solar plexus. On your return, wash your hands and face in cold water, paying particular attention to cleansing the chakras at your wrists. Wash away the energy of others before you have anything to eat. If you have already picked up others' energy, during the act of eating you can ingest their energy and it is harder to shift.

The golden rules are:

1. Plan ahead. Use your inner instinct to 'know' definitively yes or no how the energy will be for you on the night. If you have doubt, just say 'No, thank you'.

2. Pace yourself by conserving energy for 2 or 3 days before you go out.

3. When you are out, use your inner monitor to observe your warning flags that you are starting to tire.

4. Speak up and tell others that you are starting to tire. I learned to give them a time frame, for example, 'I'll need to leave in 15 minutes.'

5. Wash away the residue of others' energy in cold water, as soon as you return, from your forehead, wrists and hands.

6. If possible, lie down for half an hour in a quiet room to recover your energy levels.

Other people's disbelief made me remember that when I was younger (so much younger than today – ha!) I hated, above all things, not to be believed. But here I found myself repeatedly facing the disbelief and distrust of others who expected me to perform in a particular way. And here is one of the blessings to be found in having CFS. It gives you the chance to give up on your own extreme reactions – it's just too damn exhausting. Extraneous reactions have to go. Nowadays I surprise myself with how little I care whether I'm believed or not. I can even smile (compassionately) about how I was before and realise how far I have come.

Guilt is the hardest emotion to cope with. That I should and could help out weighs heavily. I know that I might be coming across as a number one selfish bitch because people were able to rely on me before. In my full health, I was more than happy to be useful and helpful. But a long return to health, with the hindsight of knowing just how much energy I can safely expend and experiencing so much backward sliding when I just did too much, has taught me to pace myself with wisdom and temperance.

So now, yes, I do have a more self-orientated approach. It's me that has to pay the price of over-exertion. I know all too well the limitations I have. And I'd rather keep myself calm and rested in order to fulfil all the things I'd like to do with my life. So be it.

I am not the daughter, mother, grandmother, friend, partner, sibling which I was previously. This has been a really hard thing for others to understand. When they see the effect of a slump (ashen face, wandered eyes, dizziness rendering me unable to complete sentences, tearfulness, arms crossed or panicky to get home from a venue...) they might understand. I know there's not much to see. The sheer eternity of hours and days afterward where I'm left lying in my own bed unable to do much of anything, only my mother knows. She has been dedicated and stalwart throughout and I am grateful to her for picking up the pieces for me. I am so fortunate that her health is great because I wouldn't be able to count the number of times when she's had to physically care for me.

So I hope you have a significant compassionate helper in your life. You'll need it. They are your rock against all the other hard reactions you'll experience. I never feel that I let my mother down, although I often say no to her invitations to events; she understands how much I can slump and she supports me in staying strong and being 'selfish' for my own good.

Most of all, I'm grateful to the lesson in Compassion, in all the many forms which this presents itself. Compassion is the key in distancing yourself from guilt, reactive judgements and hurt. This is not a passive state of being. Instead compassion is a strength and holds to the belief that we are all the same. All one in spirit. How you feel is how I feel. Compassion breaks down the barriers instead of building more bricks in the walls between us. Did you really feel safer behind that wall? Perhaps after all, it's our own responsibility to feel safe, to detach from feeling hurt and release old reactive states of being and feel safe as ourselves. Did you really like being that old person anyway?

Compassion starts, first and foremost, in you and towards you. So, now I practise detachment from what others think because I realise that I've got to be me, the real true me, the spirit that is me, underneath the surface obligations and guilt and fear of rejection. None of these reactions are actually real because they don't stem from love. Love is who and what we really are. I know that underneath it all, beyond this body, I AM LOVE. Therefore, I am compassionate when I fall short of this goal.

You've probably heard the old saying: Walk a mile in someone's shoes before you judge them. How true is that? How many times has life shown you the B-side of something which you used to do? And how it's not much fun on the receiving side! All that you give out you get back (or karma). I am learning to detach from even this, the mirror technique which the universe is set up to show you. It makes me have an amused smile to myself now as the lessons become more obvious. As I have become more self-realised, the lessons are clearer and the 'karma' is replayed back to me almost instantly. Holding an internal check before acting starts to become habitual: would I like this to be played on me?

And compassion is the key to another secret. As you change yourself and seek to respond with compassion, others' reaction will be different. Remember the example of the colleague who acted like a victim and who was shunned for this response? In this invisible world of emotion and reactions to them, our response buttons are clearly visible in neon and seem to demand that others press them. Those whom we meet who have not learned the lesson of detachment and compassion can't seem to help evoking that response in you. Who can blame them? Alice in her trip to Wonderland couldn't help eating a cake labelled 'Eat me'. I'm sure we can all associate with that. This explains the habitual patterns which we find ourselves in. We've all found ourselves at one time or another saying 'Why did I do that?' or 'Why is this always happening to me?' Physical eyes see the physical body. But nothing is hidden in the world of emotions. The big secret is that when we learn to respond differently, others subtly pick up that cue. You will have muted the neon buttons so that they are no longer shouting out to be pressed.

Just keep on keeping on, dear hearts.

Take a few moments here to write down your thoughts. Think of a problem that you are presently faced with or where you find you have a 'Why me?' response to anything.

Think about your buttons (habitual reactions). Be honest with yourself. Imagine you can step outside your emotional body and observe it from other angles.

Where are your buttons located? What do they look like? Which emotional reaction are they linked with?

Think about letting go of that habitual response. Imagine how it will feel to have a non-response or to feel compassion instead. Explore how the other person will respond when you cease to re-act in the old way. Ask yourself: if I act from compassion, what would compassion do?

Imagine yourself smiling on the inside. Imagine your compassion breaking down walls within yourself. Imagine compassion creating a bridge. Explore sitting with the state of compassion and enjoying how this feels.

As you emerge from contemplation, place yourself in a blanket of compassion to maintain this state in the physical world.

Repeat this meditation each day for a week. You may uncover more emotional buttons or continue to work on releasing the same one. Compassion has a wonderful way of spilling over into our lives with a tonic effect. Happy exploration!

Affirmation:
'I am strong and compassionate as I speak my truth.'

Chapter 11

The raw food diet

I couldn't write a book about recovery to perfect health without reference to diet. In fact, a change in diet is vital to full recovery. It is interesting that when I mention this, some clients think that it is a bridge too far. I often hear a barrage of excuses such as 'I couldn't possibly do without meat/milk/...' or 'I don't have the time' or even 'I need my microwave because I need to feed two growing boys', etc.

Lots of things that are actually very unhealthy for us we are strangely attracted to or even addicted to. In fact, the foods we would least like to give up are often the very ones which are not good for our body. For me, this was cheese. I would find myself craving it, cutting chunks off the block. It took me years to recognise the instant signs which my body gave me indicating my allergy, which were my throat closing, wheezing and tightness in my chest, a runny nose and the next day, a migraine. It's amazing that before I cottoned onto the problem, I salivated at the thought of crackers and cheese. However, when in your head you link up the problem food and associate it with the horrible side-effects instead of the pleasure of a tasty food, it becomes a non-food that you can more easily learn to avoid. I have taught myself to wear blinkers when I'm food shopping and make a bee-line in the store for the foods I can eat. Everything else I avoid because any of the foods which have toxic reactions are no longer classed as food to me. It can take a bit of retraining yourself, but it is possible, I assure you.

Take time to reflect here for your journal.

Which food, or foods, do you already know that don't suit your body? Write down each food and beside it your specific body reaction to it. Ask yourself: why is it that I allow myself to eat this when I know it isn't good for me?

The aim is to change your mind-set about this food as bad for you. Draw a picture of the food alongside one of you becoming ill from it. Pictorial representation (even drawing yourself as a stickman) works really well, especially if it makes you laugh. The funnier the picture the better because it cements a memory-picture-emotion link which you are more likely to recall and act on the next time you are tempted to ingest food which you know will make you ill.

Sometimes it helps to place post-it notes as a reminder to yourself on the fridge door until you get used to living without certain foods.

So why raw food?

You are what you eat. I'm sure you've heard that before. But let's really look at that statement.

Scientists will tell you that matter doesn't exist. Everything which appears solid is, in fact, made up of light. We are light. Every cell of your body is light. When you eat food, you are eating light, nourished by sunlight. Food is filled with life energy. When you eat a food, you imbibe the energy in the food. If this food is the energy that your body needs, then you will feel healthy. If this food is not what your body needs, it interferes with your health.

If 'you are what you eat', then it stands to reason that you will feel better, brighter, on quality, fresh organic food. Organic food is better than food grown with pesticides and artificial fertilisers because its vibratory rate is higher and it has more natural and easily assimilated vitamins and minerals. Raw, living food is vegan so you avoid animal-based proteins which can cause cancer, osteoporosis and other health concerns.

Food which is raw is still alive and you ingest that life force contained in its enzymes. Cooking food destroys half of the life-giving enzymes and makes it more difficult to digest. Cooking also destroys 50–80% of vitamins and minerals in food. As long as food is only heated to 50 °C, the enzymes are not destroyed, so you can still enjoy warm food. You can also dehydrate raw food for 6–8 hours to create breads etc.

I came across *The Art of Raw, Living Food* by Doreen Virtue and Jenny Ross online and bought it straight away because it *felt* intuitively right for me. I read that eating raw food rapidly brings about health benefits. A 1992 Finnish study discovered that there were very significant health improvements among chronically ill people on an all-raw-vegetable diet for 1 week! When I started the raw food diet, by day 2, I recounted feeling lighter in my journal and just knowing this diet was going to be healing for me.

Early on, I was eating about 90% raw food and believe that it was a huge factor in me returning to health. So now, 4 years on, I still eat raw food for two meals a day. In the winter, I find I need some cooked food to give a slower release of fuel to keep me warm, such as thick broth soup, potatoes or rice pasta. I believe that some stodgy cooked food helps to keep me grounded (being an air sign).

I want to dispel two myths about raw food, namely: that preparation of raw food is too time-consuming and it requires expensive equipment. Some meals do need to be prepared in advance but if you plan ahead, like making a slow-cooking casserole, it's easy. And like anything else, you can make it as complicated or simple as you like. I tried juicing, smoothies, blending, dehydrating to make wraps and cookies and 'cakes' etc.

Smoothies are easiest: nuts require to be soaked overnight to leach out toxins in their skins, but apart from that, it's just throw in your fruit, supplements, nuts, seeds or vegetables and whizz. A meal in a minute. This is my breakfast of choice. Seeds are highly important in your new diet because they contain essential oils and omegas which are key to the healing of the brain and nervous system. As a rough guide, your breakfast should contain 2 tablespoons of linseed, 1 tablespoon of pumpkin seeds and 1 tablespoon of sunflower/sesame seeds.

Juicing is also easy but leaves you with leftover pulp. I use this pulp to make easy wraps or cookies. I suggest getting a good book or joining a raw food page on a social network to get the basic ideas. I'm sure you'll find a few favourite recipes which are quick and easy to prepare. I have included a few of my favourite easy recipes in appendix A.

Nor does raw food need to be expensive. You don't need to spend a lot of money on juicers or dehydrators. My equipment cost under £20: £9 for a hand blender from the supermarket and a second-hand juicer for £10, valued at £80 new. Your oven set at its lowest setting of 50 °C, with the door left ajar, works as an effective dehydrator to make your own breads, cookies and wraps or to marinade vegetables.

My advice is to keep it simple and prepare in advance as much as possible.

There are huge health benefits to eating raw food. Firstly, your body functions better. Your joints and nerves feel better tuned and pain free. Your brain works better and the foggy feeling is lessened. Secondly, you will feel more emotionally in tune with others around you. The extreme tiredness of fatigue can lead to a 'deadening' feeling as if you are behind a plate glass from everyone and not quite living. Raw, living food gives you its life force and lifts you back into the realms of truly living and feeling again.

This can be both a blessing and a curse at times. Sometimes I feel so open and aware that I can feel my neighbours in their houses. I have to make a concentrated effort to shut down, protect and use blinkers on my thoughts. But I think this is one of the factors of the hyper-sensitive state that Chronic Fatigue Syndrome brings anyway.

But I'm not saying that I'm a saint all the time. Sometimes when I'm out for a meal or visiting a friend, I may succumb to that tasty slice of wheat bread or a cake, but I know the consequences. I know that when I eat foods which don't agree with me, I'll feel tight across my chest and the next day my joints feel tight and I feel 'dulled down' as if I'm not so alive and alert as I am on my usual healthy raw diet. Besides, if you do break your diet, don't beat yourself up. Drink lots of water to flush your system. The next day, take a squeeze of lemon in hot water on rising. It's great for detoxing. In addition, take aloe vera juice and garlic capsules to aid the detox process.

As well as sprinkling a blend of omega-rich seeds on your breakfast, I recommend taking a high-quality omega nutritional supplement, such as 'VegEPA', which contains omegas and evening primrose oil. Researchers have found that 'Reduced energy production capacity in ME/CFS sufferers results from damaged or dysfunctional mitochondria' (Myhill, S., Booth, N.E., McLaren-Howard, J., 2009). CFS sufferers have inflamed brain and spinal column and have been found to have low levels of fatty acids, particularly EPA (eicosapentaenoic acid).

EPA also plays a crucial role in cellular communication and is particularly important for brain function and central nervous system activity. Activity of the hypothalamus, the part of the brain responsible for regulating sleep, temperature control and appetite, as well as the immune system, appears to be either hyperactive or very underactive in CFS sufferers, both of which contribute to fatigue. (http://igennus.com/health-conditions/chronic-fatigue-syndrome-symptoms)

I can't recommend this product highly enough.

Organic food is the best but if you can't get organic, soak fruit and vegetables for an hour to leach out toxins. Fill a basin of cold water with a cup of vinegar or 3 tablespoons of bicarbonate of soda. Place your fresh food in the water. After 1 hour, rinse the food. You are likely to notice a scum on the water which has come out of the food.

Blessing and giving thanks for your food will also raise the light quotient in it. Performing a ritual blessing while you prepare the food or eat it reminds you of your divine self and will remind you to tune into the divine in gratitude several times a day. This is the blessing which my mother uses to bless her food which you might like to use. Focus on feeling gratitude while you say the blessings. Visualising the journey behind the words with intent is most important:

'Divine Mother, we receive this food with gratitude. Please bless this food back to the soil in which it grew, the seed from which it grew, the sunshine and drops of rain which helped it grow, and the many hands which brought it to our plate. Amen.'

Ten golden rules of raw food

1. Buy organic fruit and vegetables if possible.
2. Have something raw at each meal.
3. If having warm food, only heat to 50 °C.
4. Drink lots of water. If your mains supply water has fluoride added, it is better to filter the water before drinking or use bottled water. Many heavy compounds in water are removed when filtered through the carbon cartridge in a household filter jug. If in doubt, check with your local water supplier.
5. Limit your consumption of caffeine. Tea, coffee and fizzy drinks have surprisingly high levels of caffeine. If you are thirsty, drinking any of these does not slake

thirst but will act as a diuretic, causing you to become more dehydrated. Also, be aware that caffeine peaks and troughs are linked to the cause of depression. Caffeine may seem to give you energy but it is a false energy which in fact robs you of your precious store.

6. Swap as many unhealthy drinks as you can for herbal teas. Or pick your own leaves to make a tisane or tea. Three or four leaves is enough. Nettle leaves make a lovely detoxing tonic; dandelion is *the* tea for bladder and urinary problems; meadowsweet flowers or leaves in tea are great for reducing inflammation; sage leaves are antiseptic and cooling on the body which helps with an over-heated brain.

7. Sweeten your food using natural sugars in fructose, stevia, honey (unless you are vegan) or agave syrup (from cactus). Sugar, like caffeine, gives instant highs but in the long run brings slumps in energy. Artificial sweeteners have a long catalogue of ill-health effects and are not advised as a replacement for sugar. Fizzy diet drinks, whether sugar or artificial sweetener based, are not recommended as part of a healthy energy-giving diet.

8. Avoid processed or pre-packed food as the life force has been reduced by the manufacturing process to very little. You might as well be eating cardboard. Remember that with new perception, food is more than the sum of its parts, more than its mere nutritional value. Food is light.

9. Avoid wheat, dairy and alcohol which have a deadening, dampening-down reaction in the body. There may be other foods such as spices or smoked food which you can add to this list.

10. Avoid animal products. You ingest the thoughts and fears of the animal as well as the antibiotics and chemicals

which were fed to the animal. Meat is much more difficult for your body to digest, which will tire your system.

Affirmation:
'I am what I eat.'

Chapter 12

Getting a good sleep

There is a mental chatter which reverberates around and within the body. This is a 'normal' state for the human existence. Or rather, it is perceived as normal, even when medical and subjective evidence clearly show to us that this isn't a healthy way to live our lives. Spiritual masters of the human experience teach us that detachment and simplicity are the keys to a happy, healthy life. Quite the opposite of how we run our lives. With all the stimulation, visual, aural, mental and emotional, it's not surprising that we flag under the constant pressure to be here, there, do this, do that, dawn till dusk. The result is a mind and body never at rest, even during sleep. If, indeed, sleep is attainable. The mind is struggling to process all the needs, wants and thoughts of the waking period. While this may be normal for us, it isn't natural and I think we need to rethink our norm.

Anyone who suffers Chronic Fatigue Syndrome knows about the mental unrest all too vividly. When the body and mind become too overstimulated, the resulting mental chatter is difficult to wade through to find peace. A state of overstimulation can be the result of too much conversation, sensory overload or too many periods without adequate rest.

In this chapter, I wish to describe the cause of 'clutter' and 'static' build-up in the body and mind. Thereafter, I will list several methods which work for me to shed this energy clutter or to break a cycle in my mind which are conducive to a good night's sleep.

Sometimes when we are busy, we don't notice the accumulation of tension. We get caught up in the fun or experience of the moment we are in, and the internal register of 'fatigue measure' or 'fatigue warning' gets overlooked. You will know what I mean: that there is a background concern, or even a fear, that you'll slip back into the helpless, spent state where everyday tasks in the world seem like an unachievable goal. Tantalisingly close but yet so far, at least for the short term. The fatigue marker is a necessary internal state where you learn through trial and error when to appoint warning flags to how you feel. For example, when I feel I am talking just too much and everyone else thinks I'm doing well, I realise that I've got sort of trapped in a 'can't stop talking mode'; this is a yellow flag for me that I'm starting to get tired, although I'm not displaying that outwardly. If I don't listen, or feel I can't get away to rest, then the next alert is that I start to go quiet. The final state is I raise a red flag when I find I've withdrawn and my arms are folded over my solar plexus to protect myself to stop any more energy leaking. At the red flag stage, others usually notice that I'm a terrible colour as my face turns ashen. At this stage, it is too late for me to do anything but to say that it is time to leave. The fun is over and there's no recourse but to leave, go home and rest quietly. The rest period after one of these turns can be anything from until late afternoon the next day to several days.

The irony is that after a state of over-exhaustion and long periods of resting, the blessed sleep to rest and recuperate, which you so obviously require, sadly can be difficult to achieve.

I was referred to physiotherapy to offer me support with my condition by putting me on a Graduated Exercise Therapy (GET) programme. The aim of this programme is to help you establish a good, balanced ratio of sleep and activity. I was told that my poor sleep pattern was the result of too much rest during the waking period (daytime). I was encouraged to keep a sleep diary for a 24-hour period for two weeks, by using four different-coloured pencils to record daily activities on the chart. Each colour represents either a period of sleep (yellow), eating (red), light activity (green) or strenuous activity (blue) on the chart. It's up to you to decide what designates a light or strenuous activity.

I recorded visits to the doctor or vacuuming as strenuous activity. Each activity is in 15-minute blocks on the chart. For example: preparing a meal (green or blue, depending on the task or how I felt that day), 15 minutes; eating a meal (red) 30 minutes; rest (green) 30 minutes; sleep (yellow) 1 hour etc.

I also recorded the breaks in my nightly sleeping pattern, for example: sleep (yellow) 1 hour 30 minutes; toilet (green) 15 minutes; sleep (yellow) 1 hour; awake unable to sleep (green) 30 minutes; sleep (yellow) 45 minutes; awake unable to sleep (green) 1 hour; eating (red) 15 minutes; awake unable to sleep (green) 45 minutes; sleep (yellow) 2 hours etc.

The result of charting my sleep really surprised me. I had known that my sleep was erratic, but when I kept a detailed record of it I could see that on some nights I was awake 14 times. A good night was when I was only awake 4 times.

Then I studied the results of my sleep chart to try to decide why I had slept poorly on some nights. This was difficult to pinpoint at first. However, I could see that a direct correlation between the days when I was very active and those when I rested a lot had an impact on how well or how poorly I slept. The days when I had exerted myself heavily, sometimes I slept well (waking 4–7 times in the night) and sometimes I woke 10–14 times in the night and had a long wakeful period of 3 hours in the middle of the night. I decided that how well I slept was the result of the type of strenuous activity I had done that day and how late in the evening or how early in the morning it had taken place. Mornings were a no go for me but sometimes I was required to attend various medical appointments in the morning. Being up and about before I felt fit had a knock-on effect for the day, and for my night's sleep.

Similarly, if I was chatting with people or in a public place, especially in the evening beyond 10 pm, I became stressed and overtired. In order to have time to unwind and cleanse myself after meeting people, I needed to be home alone before I was too depleted from all the activity to commit properly to my energy-cleansing routine (chapter 5). When I became overtired and so was unable to cleanse, I had to just tumble into bed. Those nights were the ones where sleep eluded me most. It was as if everyone's energy were jumping around inside me. It made me feel agitated: the polar opposite of the optimum condition required for sleep.

When overtired, I also experience 'jumpy leg' problems. The nerves in the legs give a spasm every 2 or 3 minutes which stops you falling asleep. I have observed that the 'jumpy leg' symptoms start as I am tiring, as if my lower half is starting to fall asleep and shut down even while the rest of me is still awake. It is one of my markers that it is time for bed. If I can arrest activity and get quickly to bed at this stage, it won't develop to be too severe. However, if I don't respond to this marker, the leg spasms become increasingly severe until I am forced to comply. Unfortunately when the spasms are severe, it takes over an hour for them to calm down once I'm in bed and so I become increasingly overtired while I try to sleep.

I recommend that you record your own sleep/activity diary (appendix B) over a fortnight period. Mark your activities into approximately 15-minute blocks, which split each hour segment into quarters. Use four colours to delineate strenuous activity, light activity, eating, and sleeping. Don't be too hung up on whether an activity is strenuous or light because this is purely subjective to your own experience. For instance, resting but not sleeping is recorded as light activity. Brushing your hair could be light or strenuous based on how this is for you on that day. Meeting a friend for coffee could be recorded as light activity, if the visit were short, but could be perceived as strenuous if it tired you excessively. Try to record each entry as soon as you can after the event, rather than trying to recall all your activities at the end of the day. It can be helpful to make short notes of your activities, in addition to the colour record on the chart, which can help you jog your memory when it comes to analysing your results.

Once you have completed your 14-day sleep diary, have a look at the results. Does anything stand out in your results? What are the precursors to those nights when you slept well? What was happening prior to going to bed on those nights when sleep was elusive? When was the activity period that day: early in the day or just prior to bedtime?

Did you have a day of light activity or strenuous activity?

Did you feel stressed at any point during the day?

Which is most tiring for you: physical exertion or interacting with people?

Did you rest for long periods during the day?

Did you get a good night's sleep the previous night or was there a knock-on effect into the next day?

At which points in the day did you eat?

Did you eat when you were hungry?

When was your first meal – was it too late or early for your metabolism?

When was your last meal of the day – was it too late or early for you?

Did you feel sleepy after any meals?

When were your snacks? Did they give you energy or not?

Did you get out into nature during the day?

Did you go for a walk?

When were you outside?

What effect did having a walk have on your sleep later that night?

I found several methods which work to aid an elusive sleep. Armed with the assessment of your sleep diary results, here are a few methods which you could try to help you sleep:

1. Eat when you feel hungry but don't eat too much as this will tire your body.
2. Don't eat too late in the evening as this will mean that you will still be digesting food when it's time to go to sleep.
3. If you have a busy schedule or physical activity one day, plan to have a quiet and nurturing evening, such as taking a bath.
4. If you have a lot of conversation but very little physical activity in a day, take a short 5–10 minute walk so that you discharge all of the 'chatter' energy down into the ground. It will also help you to change your brain waves into a state more conducive to sleep.
5. Take a warm bath with salt in it to cleanse your energy field prior to sleep.
6. If your legs are 'jumpy' or your mind is jumpy causing you to have very little rest, place your feet in a basin of cool, salty water. Rest there for 5–10 minutes. Ask the water to absorb and draw out all the toxins in your body. Imagine the water turning dark as toxins leach out into the water. Rinse your feet in fresh water.
7. Have fresh new sheets, preferably fresh off the washing line. Crisp, clean-smelling linen is conducive to a good sleep.
8. Lie on your back and imagine roots growing from your tailbone into the earth below. Discharge down into the earth all energy that is not yours. Lying on your back seems to help with releasing. Curling in foetal position tends to lock unwanted energy in your system so take time to consciously relax on your back before rolling onto your side.

I taught myself self-hypnosis when I was cramming for exams and needed to sleep. The aim is to find the most tired part of your body and to sink into it. Your head is likely to be very busy inside so it is better to release down into your body instead, to take your seat of awareness out of your head. Let go and sink further as you count down. It really works but needs a bit of patience to practise. Please keep trying though.

Self-hypnosis for sleep

Find the most tired place in your body. It could be the small of your back, your legs or your feet. Instead of holding on tight, imagine letting go and relaxing.

Keeping your seat of awareness in your tired area, start to countdown 10 to 1 in your head. Imagine that each number brings you to a deeper and quieter place within yourself.

Don't allow your attention to wander...keep your attention in the tired part of your body.

If you have reached 1 but haven't achieved sleep, start the count again 10 to 1. Imagine going down steps as you count, each step taking you deeper into peace and sleep.

Repeat the countdown 10 to 1 as many times as you need, but don't allow your sleepiness to dissipate. Instead, *keep your level of sleepiness and start the new count from there*, building on it as you count.

Self-hypnosis really works but it requires a few weeks of practice. You have all the time in the world to practise... Sleep well!

Affirmation:
'I will sleep deeply and awaken restored and refreshed.'

Chapter 13

Arrhythmia: the message of the heart

An erratic heartbeat or heart palpitations, called arrhythmia, are symptoms which can be experienced by those with Chronic Fatigue Syndrome. The heart feels as if it beats out of step for a few beats. It beats too hard and too fast and can seem to flip over, like a dying fish flapping in the chest, bringing light-headedness in its wake. This can be accompanied by a sensation that you may lose consciousness.

Arrhythmia is caused by a high level of stress, corresponding surges in adrenalin and over-exertion over a prolonged period without having access to your usual rest. Funnily enough, the erratic heartbeat does not often happen while the stressful activity is taking place. Instead, arrhythmia occurs later just as you are starting to unwind and relax. It is a delayed reaction to doing too much.

For me, these symptoms came 3 years after the initial onset of CFS. Out of the blue, just when I was thinking myself cured, arrhythmia floored me. I was in a panic. I thought that I was having a heart attack. I had pains and numbness down my left arm and into my left foot. I called for emergency attention in a state of alarm. The paramedics recorded my heartbeat and rate on a portable ECG. My heart rate was high but my blood pressure was low, hence the feeling of faintness. I was hospitalised for 2 days to monitor my heart and while the doctor tried to diagnose the cause. In the end, no cause was found. I was told that my arrhythmia was the result of CFS.

On an experiential level, I gauge these heart symptoms as a new 'flag' which marks when I have exerted myself too much. As my pacing skills have developed, I am able to avoid many of the other symptoms and have even forgotten that I had CFS. My most recent awareness is to be mindful that my body can still be overtaxed if I do too much. To be honest, this happens so seldom, it is easy to forget how I once struggled to complete daily tasks.

Since that hospital visit, I have experimented with various ways of doing self-healing on myself during the arrhythmia episodes. An erratic heartbeat can be a bit scary. If the symptoms worsen to pain or numbness in the arms or legs, it can be difficult to quell the rising panic. Panicking would be the least helpful response, as it only worsens the symptoms, causing adrenalin to flood the bloodstream.

When I had a racing heartbeat, I tried placing my hands on my heart and focusing self-healing in quiet attention, but my heart rate didn't slow or settle down. I tried placing my hands on my abdomen and sending healing to my adrenal glands. I called in the healing angels to give me healing. I focused on allowing the light and peace to flow from my hands. Mentally, I directed my intention by saying 'Peace...peace...slow' to my adrenal glands, not only saying the words but feeling the peace.

Practising self-healing worked well for slowing the body's production of adrenalin, but the heart palpitations still didn't settle. The more I focused on my heart, the more concentrated the palpitations became. Then I recalled a law of the Universe, The Law of Attention. The Law of Attention states that: *Whatever you give attention to manifests.* In other words, whatever you focus on increases.

So I tried taking my thoughts and attention out of the equation. I moved my seat of consciousness away from observing my heart. However, wherever I moved my awareness to in the body, my heartbeat was still my number one focus. So I realised that I needed to take my awareness out of the body. The solution was to take myself out of the back of my head at the point where hair spirals from your crown. Here I could 'rest' above and behind my head, allowing a complete handover of my body to its own self-healing. Here I found a quiet state of bliss. A period of disassociation from the body for a short term of 20 or 30 minutes, in a state of trust, helped my palpitations to gradually slow and my heart to return to normal.

The message from this is that my thoughts and emotions had become toxic to my heart. Every thought is experienced by the heart as if it is happening in the present moment. My physical heart could no longer cope with the harshness of mental focus or the fears that I was experiencing. Taking my seat of consciousness out of the physical body enabled my physical body to reset itself.

Take a moment here to reflect. Where are you presently looking out on the world from? Are you in your head? Are you above your head? Are you in your chest?

For most people, they find that their seat of consciousness sits above and slightly to one side of their head. Observe where you are looking through your eyes from.

Imagine your heart. Where are you looking down from? Can you sit wholly in your heart and look out from there? Play with moving your seat of consciousness. What does it feel like to look up into the body from the big toe, for example?

The above exercise is to familiarise you with observing your habitual seat of awareness in relation to the physical body.

The next exercise is to practise moving consciousness through the *bindi* point (where the hair spirals from the scalp) and observe the body from behind and above. It involves a level of detachment from the physical body. Just as in the sleep state, the physical body can rest and recover during this process.

Imagine yourself protected and connect with the earth with your grounding cord.

Call in your healing guides and angels to give you healing.

Take your seat of consciousness to the back of your head.

Observe your heart. Now detach from thinking about your heart.

Imagine you are travelling up through the back of your crown.

Sit behind and above your head.

Focus on the peace here.

Allow any thoughts of your heart which filter into your state of peace, to flow away again without attachment.

Remain in this peaceful place until you feel your physical body coming to a state of ease.

With Chronic Fatigue Syndrome, you become hyper-aware of how your thoughts and emotions influence your body. Each thought triggers a raised beat of the heart – a heart which is already taxed just to lie there and beat in your chest. Instead it seems a great effort for it just to beat and breathe.

You become aware of how each thought, with its attached emotion, sends your heart beating overtime and the corresponding hormonal responses throughout the body. And it hurts. Your heart can feel taxed by the effort of thinking. So you learn to detach from thoughts. All my meditation training would come into practice. Detach from each thought. Don't follow it or allow any emotional attachment or emotional hurt – just watch it go – like watching scenes from the window of a train (I recall a Robert Louis Stevenson poem, 'From a Railway Carriage': ...*and there is the child...and there is the green for stringing the daisies...painted stations whistle by...*). Just observe each thought and allow it to pass.

Thoughts are running through either plans for the future or scenes from the past. Whatever you become absorbed in thinking, your body reacts as if it's happening in the present moment. Only it isn't. Remember that in the present moment there is peace and ease. Your heart remembers that and can rest in the present moment. The past you cannot change. The emotional hurt which arose from a past situation, however, can be changed.

So what is the message of the heart?

Anger at another, focused through your heart, leads only to heart stress and an overtaxed heart. Anger forms a hard, closed-off centre in your heart. Whatever you send out, you receive back. This is the Universal Law of Reflection: as without, so within.

I was aware of a hard space in my heart when I was angry with someone. I meditated on this 'hard' space which is actually my angry self folding in on itself. I moved my conscious self within this angry space and found a 6-year-old me angry at not getting my own way. Anger was quietly consuming me instead. I opened my conscious self into this space and, with power, said: *'Enough! I hereby decree that this behaviour is no more. I open into love and light. Amen.'*

On returning to the usual seat of my conscious, I could observe that the hard space in my heart was gone. There was an 'unoccupied' space in my heart which was no longer fuelling anger from the inside.

So the message of the heart is to engage with anger by disengaging or ceasing to engage with the anger response. Anger has a way of bouncing back to hurt you who sent it. I will explore dealing with anger in the next chapter.

Affirmation:
'I release anger and bring in the light.'

Part 3

Recovery and forging
a healthier approach to life

Have I learned the lesson of my illness?
Have I learned it well?
Just when I thought I saw a through road,
It narrowed to a hell.
To pick and choose the meaning,
Like deciphering with no code,
Was it this, or that which drove me
To sink beneath the flood?

But still I try, and try again
To extract a meaning clear:
A new code to live by
To restore me back to health.

Chapter 14

Meaning of the illness

Before I reached burn-out, I was a human doing. Constantly striving to achieve more and more and the next: a life filled. I had practically no time to reflect, sit quiet and be the peace that I now know.

I recognise myself and most fellow sufferers of Chronic Fatigue Syndrome as the classic A-Type character. This type of personality tends to like stress. We tend to be very competitive and self-critical, striving towards goals but without feeling a sense of joy in our efforts or accomplishments. There also tends to be a life imbalance, characterised by a high work involvement. Type A personalities experience a constant sense of urgency, as if in a struggle against the clock. Often, we quickly become impatient with delays and unproductive time, schedule commitments too tightly, and try to do more than one thing at a time, such as reading while eating or watching television.

What I think is interesting is that Type A individuals tend to be easily aroused to anger or hostility, which they may or may not overtly express. I recognise that I had a constant irritation inside myself to get on, to move on, to get more done. Strangely, others saw me as so calm and placid on the exterior. So well-schooled and contained despite the toll of irritation tallying silently within me.

Empirical research shows that Type A personalities are more prone to a range of stress-related illnesses, including heart disease and high blood pressure (hypertension) (Friedman & Rosenman, 1959). While being a high achiever can be a positive attribute, research shows that this can have a negative effect on the subject's health. However, when you're in it, it creates its own high. There's a real buzz in feeling so busy, which I suppose is the adrenalin. It's like being an adrenalin junkie because it feels so good, so powerful. I got used to operating through adrenalin all the time. It was as if everyone else lived life in the slow lane...isn't it ironic that I was headed for that slow lane I despised so much? A position which I viewed as weak, helpless and unproductive from my unsympathetic, uncompassionate standpoint? Oh the ironies of life! Are we destined to experience all that which we criticise and focus emotion to, whether positive or negative? The Laws of the Universe decree that we draw it towards ourselves and manifest it through sheer strength of focus. Dispassion and patience now seem a much more healthy option. But try telling me that before! You would not have halted me from my path or deterred me from my predetermined objective. Still, time flat on one's back has a way of leading one to reconsider previous notions and modus operandi.

Reflect here. Have you ever spoken or thought vehemently in judgement of someone or a group, only to find that same experience being played out in your life?

How did this manifest for you?

Think back to the time when you made the initial emotional judgement. Did you somehow feel or know, at the time, that this was somehow significant for you?

How much of what you subsequently experienced might have been as a result of the first event? Did you attract this experience towards you?

Make notes in your journal. This is a deep reflection which will require meditation over several sessions. Open exploration will draw the answers up from your inner self.

I have come to believe that CFS is linked to adrenal burn-out. I pushed myself to achieve so much for so long that I burned myself out. I squeezed every last drop from my adrenal glands to give me the adrenalin to keep on going, long beyond the point of normal tiredness.

It is interesting to note that some people with CFS have sensitivity to adrenalin being medically administered. This is worth mentioning to your anaesthetist if you're having an operation. Local and general anaesthetics contain adrenalin. Personally, I can feel this as my heart starts to race and have palpitations.

What was the effect on my body of living in a perpetual state of stress? Writing about M.E./CFS, Charles Shepherd says that

> any kind of stress is immediately recognised by a small gland in the brain called the hypothalamus. Brain cells inside the hypothalamus which are involved in responding to stress produce two important hormones, arginine vasopressin (AVP) and cortisol releasing factor (CRF).
>
> The main effect of acute stress is to switch on a gene which controls production of the main stimulatory hormone for cortisol, corticotrophin releasing hormone (CRH). This then instructs the adrenal glands to rapidly increase their production of cortisol, a hormone which assists the body to respond to stress in an appropriate way. Levels of CRH and cortisol rise quite rapidly then fall back to normal again. In contrast, something rather strange seems to happen to people whose lives are subjected to chronic levels of physical and mental stress. Instead of producing CRH and cortisol, the hypothalamus switches to making AVP and a normal positive response to stressful events no longer occurs.
>
> (Shepherd, C., 3rd edn, 1999)

The medical evidence shows that the way I was living my life was not normal. My body was not responding in a normal manner to stress. My norm was not the healthy hormonal response which most people would experience. On the contrary, I imagined that, like a surfer, I was riding the top of the wave. I didn't ever allow myself to ride the trough behind the wave. I was 'high', surfing effortlessly on the unstoppable force of the wave. Attempting to avoid rest or non-activity through constant striving to achieve was damaging to my system. My body had become accustomed to dealing with an unhealthy stress level.

I realised that as opposed to being in the now, in acceptance for what *is*, I was always planning the next and the next. I was living in and for a future in my mind and pushing forward with an incredible drive to achieve, often against impossible odds but highly driven to achieve. In fact, I loved the challenge of seemingly impossible odds. I ignored my body's signals because I was on a single track, fuelling my engine at full throttle from the moment I opened my eyes in the morning. It was like a drug with powerful dividends to pump out all that adrenal energy. In short, it felt good and my body was young enough to cope with all the high demands on myself. As soon as one task was completed I'd be busy working on the next. In fact, I already had it planned before the first task was complete. But I was living for a future me and not being present in the present.

Then I got to wondering if the adrenal glands, which produce adrenalin, situated at the top end of the kidneys, at the level of the solar plexus were linked with the 'disconnected' feeling between the etheric and physical body at the solar plexus which is one of the main symptoms in CFS. Could it be that the dizziness and feeling of dislocation were due to a disparity at the solar plexus? I had all the time in the world to explore this during my long rest periods.

Louise Hay, in her book *You Can Heal Your Life*, suggests many explanations for why we get illnesses. She says that those who experience:

- **Fatigue** exhibit a resistance, boredom and/or a lack of love for what they do;
- **Adrenal problems** have an issue with defeatism, no longer caring for the self and/or suffering anxiety.

I decided to 'sit' with each of these explanations to see if these made any sense to me in relation to what I was experiencing.

I have always had a low boredom threshold. I assumed it was related to a high IQ, but linking it to CFS I can see that it was part of the drive to achieve. It simply was mind-numbingly boring to me just to stand still. I considered it a waste of time to not be productive by one means or another for even a minute.

It makes perfect sense to me that resistance is listed as a key factor in Fatigue because, in addition to feeling bored extremely easily, I was resistant to either sitting still or to others wasting both my time and theirs. Why prevaricate? Just get on with it, I would think! With that came an irritation towards others. I found it easier just to do everything myself than to take time to explain how to do it to another, then watch them take forever to complete the task. As such, my demands on others as well as myself were often unreasonable. It is only with the gift of hindsight that I can see that these were unhealthy approaches, akin to OCD. I had thought it was a healthy disregard for the products of my labours which led me to continually move to work on the next creative project. But was this a healthy detachment? Now, I can see that perhaps some pause to celebrate my achievements was not only allowable but perhaps healthier. So, Louise Hay's explanations for fatigue, of resistance, boredom and a lack of love for what I did, were a perfect match for how I had led my life. I could associate with them all.

Since I was mulling over the idea of adrenal fatigue, I decided to 'try on' Louise Hay's observations on adrenal problems for size. How well did they fit my own problems? This was harder to identify with. I have rarely felt defeated, never mind defeatism (Pollyanna hadn't been defeated – neither would I!). However, I saw that the other two observed character traits, 'not caring for the self' and 'suffering anxiety', were not to be so easily dismissed. Is it anxiety, this irritation? This itching drive to push ahead? Is this anxiety? It's not the classic gnawing anxiety of fear which I would have associated with anxiety. But it did create a stress in the body, this constant pushing ahead for more, to do more, to achieve more, more, more, more. All of which, I just knew, secretly and quietly within myself, meant I wasn't being kind to me. I will explore more on kindness towards oneself in chapter 17.

Take a moment here to reflect and make notes in your journal.

How do Louise Hay's meanings for why the body manifests a disease or illness fit you?

Fatigue:

- Are you resistant to the message of your body?
- Do you express what you are feeling?
- Are you bored easily? Why?
- Do you feel stuck in a dead-end position?
- Do you love what you do? Or is there some unexpressed wish for something which you'd rather be doing?

Adrenal problems:

- Do you feel defeated? Do you feel powerless to change your circumstances?
- Do you feel that your health is secondary to the goal which you are setting out to achieve?
- Are you anxious? Are you stressed? In which area of your life do you feel anxious/stressed?

Have a dialogue with yourself in your journal regarding any fresh understandings you uncover. Do you need to explore changing your attitude to the situation? Or are there external changes which you need to make in your world?

Make a list of changes which you will make to improve your

circumstances. Select one at a time to work on over the next few weeks. Write your progress through use of an ongoing inner dialogue in your journal.

At a later date, it may be worthwhile revisiting the questions above to explore if there are additional changes you'd like to make.

CFS has taught me to be still and rest in the present moment. To accept what I am experiencing right now. It's been a real eye-opener because instead of being in a lesser state than my fast-track doing, with the power of Acceptance, living in the present is so intensely self-fulfilling!

And so in my quiet acceptance, I became aware that I was experiencing a physical and energy body disparity, as if they were out of sync. Through healing training, I knew about the seven bodies that we inhabit like the layers around an onion, with the physical body being the innermost, composed of dense matter. In truth, all of these bodies, the mental, emotional, etheric body double, spiritual body etc., are light which vibrates at different rates overlapping around and through one another. I got to thinking that the out-of-sync feeling and the dizziness/nausea could be due to a disparity in vibratory rate between different bodies, as if they didn't quite connect properly or were not in harmony.

Use your internal vision.

How does your solar plexus feel? From the front? From the back? From the inside?

Do you feel 'connected'?

Is there a sense of disconnection? If so, where does it stem from?

Explore the root of feeling connected/disconnected.

Ask yourself: what do I need?

So, in meditation, lying down prone on the bed, I placed my hands on my abdomen and 'tuned into' my etheric energy body, which vibrates just beyond the skin of the physical body. It felt to me as if it didn't quite connect with the physical body at the solar plexus. Lying down flat on my back with my hands on my abdomen, I concentrated on reconnecting and settling my bodies again using the power of intention. I breathed into my solar plexus with my hands on the abdomen holding the focus of my concentration, imagining filling my solar plexus with golden light until I felt better.

Meditation to reconnect your energy bodies at the solar plexus

Lie quietly on your back. Use your protective method and ground down into the earth.

Call in your healing guides and angels to help with the intent of attuning your bodies at the solar plexus.

Place your hands on your solar plexus. Breathe quietly and allow yourself to experience how you feel at the solar plexus. Imagine breathing in white light. Breathe out 'grey' and release it to the trees or the earth. Repeat until you feel calm and filled with light.

Imagine looking into your solar plexus with your inner vision. Ask to 'see' the connection between the physical and etheric bodies. How does it look? Feel?

Breathe in white light directly into the solar plexus. 'Charge' it with light. Imagine that light bridging the connection between the bodies, bringing them into harmony. Keep 'charging' your solar battery until you feel strong and vital.

'Discharge' old energy down into the earth through an imaginary lightning rod.

Keep running white light. Breathe in white light; discharge the grey into the earth.

To close, place one hand over the other hand at the solar

plexus. Imagine placing a shielding disc over it, in whichever form springs to mind for you. Whatever you think is real for you.

The message of the solar plexus is that living in a constant state of irritation or anger is not a healthy way to be. It has physical, mental and spiritual repercussions for your whole being. Anger is a great destroyer. It destroys the peace within you and floods you full of adrenalin.

Choose to defuse this anger. A simple and effective method is to cross your arms and firmly stroke down from your shoulders to below the elbows a few times. This releases oxytocin, the 'love hormone', which is a natural relaxant and counteracts adrenalin.

If you find yourself consumed with anger, instead of blaming others, choose to deal with it. A great way to deal with anger is to go for a walk, sit in a garden or just be in nature once a day. Use conscious awareness to discharge anger down into the earth below your feet.

Imagine you have a lightning rod from the soles of your feet, channelling your anger, like an electric current, down to be recycled. Focus on *release*. Holding onto anger avails nothing but a destructive energy contained inside. Instead, let go. Breathe in the air and peace around you. Nature lives only in the present moment. Each bird that sings or plant that grows expresses itself to its utmost within this moment. We can learn a lot from the conscious simplicity of natural living things.

Affirmation:
'I release anger and choose to feel peace.'

Chapter 15

Acceptance

At some point in the journey, you will reach the point of acceptance. After all the fight with the illness, the tears, the 'Why me?', despair, grief, loss and pain, this is the most healthy point to reach. The turning point in the healing process. Acceptance tells your soul that now you are ready to listen. For me, over time, all the anguish and despair eventually settled out into a calm, quiet resignation to the condition that I found myself experiencing. I won't say I was 'suffering', but it was simply what I perceived that I was experiencing.

Around this time, I realised that I had a choice in how I perceived this condition. I could continue to rail and wail against it, like King Canute's futile attempt to prevent the incoming tide by sheer force of his will against nature. Similarly, I could also choose to experience more suffering by using my energy reserves to fight the diagnosis or continue to identify with the diagnosis. Or I could rest quietly in a state of acceptance and let the experience teach me its own lessons. Choosing to experience this state as suffering is just that, a choice. Instead, I chose to think positively about my condition. It was different and more physically limiting but what were the blessings within it? Pollyanna in the famous eponymous children's classic by Eleanor H. Porter when faced with all manner of setbacks, including loss of the use of her legs, still chose to find something to be glad about. I like that. To a certain extent, a positive outlook despite the situation has always been my approach. I'd rather play Pollyanna's Glad Game and find solutions than choose to wallow in the problem presenting itself to me. The more limited the options available, the more exciting I find the challenge to discover a viable solution.

Life has taught me to have a healthy attitude to change and the adaptations it brings. As our life on this planet is transient, so too do our experiences come and go. When faced with a difficult situation, my grandmother used to ask me, 'Do you think any of this will matter 5 years, 10 years, a hundred years from now?' That has always helped me get a handle on the issue being presented. Did my concern really matter? So, as regards my 'illness', I finally chose to accept the diagnosis and rest. And on my better days, I would devote myself to bringing all the tools I had learned – the meditation, the yoga breathing, the healing, positive thinking, affirmation, the raw vegan diet, prayer, blessings, gratitude, herbal and homeopathic medicinal knowledge – to bear on bringing myself back to full and perfect health.

Viewed from a higher awareness, your condition has been given to you, or you have chosen it, like me, to experience some part of ourselves. In a quiet state of rest and acceptance, I became aware of the effect of each thought on my physical and emotional and mental bodies. You, too, are in the fortunate position of having a heightened awareness of how each thought is being felt and experienced in the physical body in each moment. Just think: others without your sensitivities or gifts, if you choose to see the condition as such, can continue to act and think unconsciously, but you are being shown minute upon minute that life is a conscious process and we are creating our reality around us with every single thought. What a gift that irrefutable knowledge truly is! You will now *know* that you are not the physical body. Also, you will know that neither are you the thoughts which your mind generates. Nor are you the emotions which churn up in the body to be translated into physical symptoms. You can still the mind, calm the emotions and know that you are peace. You are deeper, older, and wiser than the symptoms of Chronic Fatigue Syndrome themselves. You are separate from the condition. How could those three words somehow define the sum and total of you? You are greater than the sum of your parts. I realised that inert wisdom in my being was starting to speak to me in these quiet moments of meditation when I was receptive and accepting. All within and around you simply *is*. Without judgement, blame, guilt or fear of reprisals, all simply exists.

I find mantra a good vehicle to touching that irrefutable peace within: *'I am that I am'* repeated in a singing chant with an open mind, until the experiential shift is experienced within yourself.

You will experience that you are separate from your bodies. Emotions are the language of the soul. I would take the time to listen to your soul that may be speaking to you from that howl of anguish, that whisper of not feeling good enough, that despair of feeling a victim, that heavy guilt of being a disappointment that you carry. Any of these present you with a valuable opportunity to grow, to find out who you are and find out your life purpose. You have been stopped dead in your tracks to assess life's meaning. Just think, did you have a chance to think, to reflect on who you were when you were busy 'doing' all the time? I loved being busy to the extreme. I believed that my short meditations every day, saying a few mantras, doing my yoga practice most days and volunteering a big chunk of my time in a local environment group was me being spiritual and connected on my path. How naive I was. In my heart of hearts, I knew I wasn't quite touching on my path, my innermost connection with who I was. But how could I find the time? I was busy bringing up a family, working full time, teaching yoga and focusing on a million other tasks and many distractions from connecting with my innermost self. The truth was that inside myself I was never at Peace. I was always pushing myself to the next and the next and the next under constant stress.

I remember watching a documentary following the life of a Christian monk who lived a very simple existence. The camera filmed him washing his few dishes in a basin out on the veranda. He explained that he was maintaining single-pointed focus on the task at hand: how the water felt, the conscious washing of each dish with a cloth, the rinsing and laying aside to dry. He did not allow his thoughts to deviate to anything else. I was moved by his simple demonstration of how conscious living could be. I tried this task when I was doing dishes and, at that time, I found it impossible. If I was lucky, I might maintain focus for 10 seconds! But mostly I was only able to focus for 1 or 2 seconds. It drew me up short and made me realise that I was kidding myself if I thought I was on the path of inner peace. I had a long way to go!

On another level, this also impressed upon me how much we affect others – that monk would never know how his humble sharing had affected me. And so I also realised that we can never know how a passing remark can be taken. From this I came to trust that the power of words, spoken with an intention to help and heal, can transform or be just the right thing that others need to hear at that time. We can never know. My resulting belief is that we should act with others' best intention at heart at all times. You might just spur that epiphany of understanding. The Eureka Moment. A leap of consciousness. How lovely that would be!

And nor should we have to know the effect of our conscious words or actions. I believe that the healing seed was received by the person whether they know it or not. And most importantly, whether we know it or not. The power of intention to uplift another's spirits is enough. On our part, once spoken, detach from the results. We can all recall chance meetings with someone which sparked a chain of events and a new consciousness, sometimes months or years after the meeting. So now I trust that process. I speak the words intuition bids me to say and bless the other person as they go on their way. A seed has been sown which may lie dormant or may sprout into life if it is the right thing on their life path.

I know that in the past I would have had to have had messages from the Divine come to me from several sources before I would trust the significance for me. If it came three times, then I'd act on it. Then I got to thinking: why wait for three calls? I decided to trust the Divine guidance if I realised that I just *knew* when the message was important. It would feel like I got a clear yes or no in the navel chakra, my internal sounding board. I can certainly say it makes life easier when you have developed your own divination tool!

Acceptance can at first glance be seen as a static, passive viewpoint, but in actual fact it is a very dynamic status. This is when your true healing starts. I meet a lot of M.E. and CFS sufferers who are extremely angry to have this condition, about their loss of capability, and display hostility when offered an alternative healing approach. What I say to them is: I invite you to change that viewpoint to see if, in the selection of an alternative approach, you find the calm within the storm, if you find the eye in the needle point of existence. You are free to reconnect and continue with your previous viewpoint, if you so choose it. However, I would invite you to lay this aside and to wear the garment of acceptance. Perhaps you could imagine sloughing off the angry jacket for a while? Try to view the exterior world and all the people in your life through the blanket of acceptance. It involves work. No easily swallowed, bitter pill from the GP (how many of us were offered anti-depressants?). And it involves more than your participation but an intention to change.

So the self starts to speak to you in the language of feelings...which can be overlooked until the message becomes more and more insistent that something is wrong here. It was only when I was floored that at last I had time to think. I believe that you, like me, are becoming more sensitive so that you can experience and thereby 'know' that you are soul.

When you drop all the fight to continue to do, think, feel as you once did, a wonderful quiet, calm acceptance comes over you. I believe that this was always on the cards for you: a time allotted to you to reflect and grow, to reflect and let go, honing and fine-tuning your thoughts, expectations, reassessing who you thought you were and to at last realise who you are. And be deeply grateful for the chance to rest. And be deeply grateful for the chance to get to know you at last.

And in that quiet acceptance comes true healing, once the perception is laid aside that we are the physical body or that we are victims in life's lottery. Acceptance brings its own peace. This is where you are right now. I invite you to lay the book aside, look inside yourself and do a 'spring clean'. Do you have outdated, overused reactions which really don't serve you now? Why hold onto them? Honest self-enquiry is often surprising: more entertaining and so much more worthwhile than a drama on TV!

Write down anything you wish to let go of on a piece of paper.

Choose one of the elements to transmute the emotion into a higher vibration. Inviting the element to transmute emotions you wish to release is even more effective.

Fire can be a very cathartic purifier if you symbolically burn the paper, allowing the remains to blow away as smoke (air element).

You could use the element of earth to recycle the energy if you bury the paper and other symbolic objects in the soil.

Standing beside a fast-flowing river is energising at the best of times but you can use the power of the water to carry away your emotion along with your paper.

Imagine your chosen element working to cleanse you and raise you to a higher and healthier vibration. I say an affirmation like:

'I hereby release _____ (e.g. anger) for my highest good. So be it. Amen.'

'I hereby release _____ (name) to his/her highest good for my highest good. So be it. Amen.'

The power of acceptance draws consciously on the universal field of energy and manifests as a more healthy approach to life.

Useful affirmations:
'I choose to accept my condition for all it has to teach me.'
'I have perfect health.'
'I am at peace, perfect peace.'

Chapter 16

Other therapies and supplements

In this chapter I would like to discuss other therapies which I tried in my endeavour to recover my health and how effective these were for me. Cognitive behavioural therapy (CBT) and graded exercise treatment (GET) were offered on the NHS (the UK National Health Service). The other alternative health therapies and treatments I explored privately. I received these over a period of 3 years with a gap of several months between each.

1. Cognitive behavioural therapy

This therapy is widely offered on the NHS. It is a behaviourist psychology approach which purports that we can be 'conditioned' to react and behave differently. It is based on the theories of a psychologist called Skinner who found that with certain reprogramming people can learn to respond appropriately to certain stimuli. Earlier work by Pavlov, a behaviourist psychologist working with dogs, found that if a bell was rung when their food arrived, they would salivate. The dogs would associate the bell with food so that when the bell was rung, even without the food being present, they would salivate.

As a person who seeks to treat the whole person as body, mind and soul, this simplistic view seeks to reduce us to the level of automatons which can be reprogrammed to function back at an efficient level. It ignores emotional and spiritual engagement with the healing process. On requesting this therapy, my GP remarked that there was no empirical evidence to suggest that this is an effective treatment for Chronic Fatigue Syndrome; nevertheless she was happy to refer me because, in her experience, some people gave anecdotal evidence that it was helpful.

I was offered an 8-week block of one-to-one time with a psychiatric nurse. I was sceptical that this would be helpful but was willing to give it a go. From the outset, I really liked my therapist and came to give him my confidence with a sense of relief that I hadn't reckoned on. It felt good to be able to talk freely about my condition when I felt that my family were fed up listening to me. It was also helpful to have him mirror back to me how positive my approach was to my own healing and how it was helping me. The slow progress of recovery can be a bit demoralising so it was lovely to be told I was doing well.

If you are offered CBT, my advice is to try it out. Success would depend on the rapport you develop with your therapist, but you may find it helpful.

2. Graded exercise treatment
Graded exercise treatment, or GET, is the other therapy which is widely offered on the NHS through physiotherapy. It is a graduated exercise programme to build up stamina and strength after a long period of convalescence. It is based on the evidence that muscles atrophy when they are not used over time and this therefore further exacerbates the feeling of 'tiredness'. The theory is that the less you do, the less you will be able to do.

I was assigned to a physiotherapist who was fairly knowledgeable about CFS. By the time I got this treatment, I had already recovered much of my physical health. I was given some advice on pacing my daily physical or mental exercise to help me get a better sleep at night.

Basically, the idea is, if my activity had been mostly social or mental in a day, then I was advised to take a 10-minute walk in the early evening. If my activity that day had been mainly physical, I was told to rest in the evening. Simple approach really but, like CBT, what is helpful is someone pointing out the obvious.

One person I know also found this a really helpful approach.

She learned to think of each daily activity in terms of energy points. If she thought of herself as having ten 'energy points' at the beginning of the day and each activity used up a number of these points, then for example, walking the dog used three points; making scones used four points; brushing her hair was one point. She placed ten beans in her pocket to represent her energy points. When all her beans were used, she had to rest. She found it helpful because it stopped her over-exerting or overtiring herself. This can be a useful approach when learning to pace your activity:rest ratio.

3. Acupuncture

I am a fan of acupuncture. I found it really helpful for various health complaints prior to being diagnosed with CFS and was hopeful that it could help. My therapist was able to observe that several of my meridian lines were low in energy by finding five different pulses at my wrist. She set about popping needles or hot cups onto various points in my body to bring up my energy levels. I am sad to say that, despite several treatments, my symptoms were only slightly improved. However, I found it positive that acupuncture boosted my energy enough for me to engage better with my own healing process.

4. Cranio-sacral therapy

I saw an advert in the local newspaper advertising osteopathy as a method of curing Chronic Fatigue Syndrome. When I went to the therapist, I found she was using cranio-sacral therapy to raise the energy levels at the base of the spine and to help me to ground better with the Earth. I was told that most people with CFS/M.E. had a difficult transition into this incarnation at birth or were resistant to being on Earth and so did not ground properly with the planet.

The therapist placed her hands under my lower spine as I relaxed on her bench. She gently stretched and vibrated the area with her hands which was very relaxing. However, after six treatments I felt no improvement.

5. Medical herbalism

I made an appointment with a medical herbalist to treat an irritable bladder and CFS. She interviewed me for an hour, linking all my health issues, before deciding on nine herbs to use as a blend. I was given these dried herbs to take as a tisane (tea), as well as these herbal essences in alcohol to be taken as 15 drops in water.

The initial dose prescribed was too strong for me as it exaggerated the fatigue symptoms and made me feel heavy. The essences in alcohol were also too strong. I have an allergic reaction to alcohol but thought I would be able to cope with 15 drops. It seems that as time goes on, my sensitivities increase, so much so that I can no longer tolerate any alcohol. On my second appointment, I related my problems with the treatment. The herbalist made up another blend for me, this time with only six herbs in it. However, even on the reduced dosage the same symptoms of heaviness and fatigue persisted. My herbalist ended up stating that this approach isn't for everybody.

However, my prior experience is that herbs are a powerful medicine. I would not discount them working well for other people.

6. Spiritual healing

I have been lucky enough to be born into a family where my mother gave us spiritual healing when we were young. I have learned that hands-on (or hands-off) healing is a natural expression of love. However poorly I felt, it always made me feel better and at peace. It was natural to use spiritual healing on my own children, even before training as a healer.

Much of this book is dedicated to practising self-healing. However, I would advise that you receive healing as an ongoing treatment to raise your light levels and to restore your energy reserves. I found this was the most beneficial treatment. A healthy sleep pattern was restored which reassured me with a deep sense of well-being that everything I was experiencing was part of my healing journey. On the days when I felt despondent, healing restored me on many levels. Over a period of time, both receiving healing and practising self-healing reset my physical and energy bodies in a deeply meaningful and fulfilling way.

7. Dietary supplements

There is some support for the role of food intolerance and sensitivities in the onset and progression of CFS symptoms. Identifying which foods may be contributing to your symptoms may be helpful in condition management and recovery. Ask your GP to run a series of blood tests to find out if you have food intolerances or nutritional deficiencies in your diet. Over a long period of living with stress, certain minerals can become depleted in your body.

I read some cutting-edge research and clinical evidence suggesting that the reduced energy production capacity in CFS/M.E. sufferers results from damaged *mitochondria* – tiny cellular structures in our cells responsible for turning food into energy. Mitochondria can be damaged or affected by toxins and stress, either mental (for example, the demands of daily life, relationships, work issues or trauma) or physiological (due to high free-radical production from everyday chemical reactions and poor nutrition).

Omega 3, specifically EPA (eicosapentaenoic acid), plays a crucial role in regulating inflammation in cell pathways. The inflammatory nature of CFS/M.E. means that the body's demand for EPA is very high and needs to be regularly replenished. I read about 'VegEPA', produced by Igennus, as a very high-standard supplement with miracle results for CFS and decided to give it a try. After 2 weeks on a dose of four capsules a day, I felt an improvement in my mental processing. After a month, the fuzzy thinking and lack of coherence in thought processes had reduced to such an amount that I felt normal for the first time in 2 years. After 2 months, I reduced the dose to two capsules a day to maintain my health and continued on this dose for 2 years. I can't recommend this product highly enough.

Conclusion

On receiving a diagnosis, there is a tendency to read widely on the subject of your condition, labelled as Chronic Fatigue Syndrome or myalgic encephalomyelitis (M.E.), and all the dire symptoms that it could hold in store for you. I do not think that this is ultimately helpful in the healing process. Associating too closely with the illness ties you into the debilitating effects. You can think yourself ill as well as thinking yourself well. Remember, the universe presents you with the external world as a mirror to your thoughts: as you think, so it is. You are at each moment creating your reality with your thoughts. This book focuses on lifting you beyond the confines of the diagnosis and seeks to empower you to step on the road to recovery with full knowledge of the power that you have to transform and to reset to your original healthy blueprint.

Similarly, listening to others with the condition in a support group or online social network page can reinforce a sense of associating with the disease. I wish to remind you that you are not the disease. Ultimately, on the road to healing, a necessary disassociation with the so-called syndrome and its symptoms is vital. Align yourself with a healthy frame of mind and perfect health. Reprogramme your physical body to the perfect blueprint of your etheric body.

Use a mantra, such as: *'I am healthy.'*

Say it, feel it, believe it, as many as 100 times day. I find it helps to place a post-it note where I will be reminded several times a day to recite the mantra. Try sticking the mantra on the wall above or opposite the toilet so that you will be reminded to recite it when you visit the loo. Or on the bathroom mirror to be viewed as you brush your teeth. Or near the kettle. Or on a wall in your bedroom. Anywhere that you can think of where you would be reminded to recite it.

Try chanting the mantra out loud or singing it. Both are particularly effective. The secret of the alchemy of healing is to imagine how it *feels* to be well. Imagine yourself doing all the favourite things you love to do, happy and in perfect health. Act as if you are in perfect health.

Affirmation:
'I am healthy.'

Chapter 17

Ahimsa (non-violence): getting the balance right

Prior to being gifted with energy sensitivity, I had been my own worst enemy. I had a need to be perfect. But that is an unrealistic and unobtainable goal. And who used to beat me up the most when I fell short of that mythical perfection? Me. All my faults were, to me, emblazoned in neon. What amazed me was that others didn't even seem to see failures which were so obvious to me. We are talking about beating yourself up for small details, minutiae: the small imperfections which others wouldn't even guess at.

The seeking to be perfect is a hard taskmaster. And not a peaceful one to sit with. In the centre of myself I cracked the whip relentlessly. So relentlessly in fact, I wore myself out over many years. One thing which you quickly find out with CFS, in the early stages, is that you have no energy for all the tasks which you'd like to do. It also exposes all your unconscious states of being. Tightness in your body is an indicator which relates loudly and clearly to your 'holding on' to what is no longer good for you. Tightness is the past speaking to you in the voice of fear, mostly fear of being not good enough.

So here I came to the realisation: what if... ('What if' is a great game to play – it steps you out of the 'box' you've chosen to inhabit and allows you to imagine, therefore create, new solutions or ways of Being!)

What if...you use your willpower to defocus from your faults and pan back to focus on all the wonderful aspects of that project or task which *had* gone right?

What if...we allow ourselves to sit within small failures and accept them? Perhaps even to find that there is perfection in all things? And come to realise that so-called 'imperfections' may merely be a result of our flawed perception.

I know that in those moments when I take myself beside a flowing stream to sit and soak in the hush of nature, I become absorbed first in the sights around me. All the glowing colours, the drape of those branches, the dapple of light reflected from the water to the underside of the overhanging foliage. Then my other senses overtake sight. The rich smells and the damp river air in my nostrils. A sound of rustles by a foraging creature or a bird raises my eyes skyward, observing the filter of light from above. My attention is drawn to the orchestra of deep, high or musical tones arranged by the water as it tumbles over the rocks, and I am absorbed. At some point I close my eyes just to listen and, when I open them again, find I am transfixed by all the beauty around me. And the perfection of it all. How each leaf, stone, sound is *perfect*! And in the haphazard way they lie, I find the glory of perfection. Nothing needs to be added. All is simply perfect and wonderful for it, just as it is.

Could we find that appreciative perfection in our own creations? After all, the creative process involves that which is created actually evolving naturally and organically. So the 'fault', if there is one, is not with the product, but with the perception of fault.

I decided that a healthy, loving me would let go of extreme judgement. I would try to create without holding onto preconceived, rigid expectations of how it should turn out. Perhaps what we create sort of gets a life of its own? We only offer the vehicle of its creation. How it eventually turns out is organically how it will.

Detachment. That is the healthy lesson: acceptance and a healthy detachment from results of our labours.

Take time to reflect here.

So Let Go and Accept.

Appreciate the talents you have which allow you to conceive and complete a project. From that small planted pot or garden, to that beautiful meal or that patchwork cushion.

Be grateful.

Practise gratitude for the gifts and skills you have, the time and materials needed to express those gifts, guidance and support you've had over the years to develop those skills, and gratitude for the objects of your labours.

Know that when you feel gratitude you are drawing more of that quality towards you. Like begets like.

Finally, feel gratitude for those who have benefited from your skills and things you have created.

Be kind to yourself and trust. You are guided on this path of life. You are never stumbling along blindly. It can only seem like that at times. Listen to the messages that you are being given. Learn to see the guidance being offered to you at all times, especially when things appear dark. Remember it is always darkest before the dawn.

We are spirit first and human second. We have come from our true home in spirit, to work here in a human incarnation to learn to love ourselves and others. However, in incarnating here, most of us forget the mission statement we came to achieve as we take on a heavy human body. It's a bit like losing one of our senses, where we have to grub along blindly in the dark. But not without help.

A long time ago, I learned that the universe was speaking to me in seemingly random ways and coincidences: a chance word with someone can spark something in yourself which you just *know* is important. You are free to choose to ignore the promptings if you wish. But if the life message is important to your mission statement, the same message will visit you again from another source. My golden rule is: If I get the message coming to me three times, I act on it without further question.

Like the message of Raw Food which was a seed planted by a young man I had talked to at a yoga course about his raw diet. With opportune timing, just months before the momentous change in health that was to happen to me, another friend described her raw food approach and watered the idea in my mind. Finally, I came across *The Art of Raw, Living Food* by Doreen Virtue and Jenny Ross and bought it straight away. Guided again or what? I wrote in my journal at the time:

> My work feels a toxic environment to me. I don't think it's just stress, I think it's all meant to guide me on a new path…So the book arrived yesterday in the post and my reawakening of my body begins…

Ahimsa is a non-harming attitude to others and yourself. In adopting non-violence, primarily we are focusing on being kind to ourselves. If we are kind to and with ourselves, that automatically spreads out as compassion and understanding to others. When we are no longer concerned with that aggressive self-hounding to push on, achieve or drive forward, a kinder aspect will enter our lives.

Learn to take the foot off the throttle. Whatever gets done will be done in its own time. Trust that it will get done in the right time and in the right way. Learn to trust a natural unfoldment of your expression of your tasks in such a way that they organically emerge in their own time frame.

You are learning to live and pace yourself to a different beat. The quiet beat of self-kindness. *How* you do the task is more important than what you produce. This is significant, so I'll reiterate that: being in a state of internal peace while you are working means more than finishing the job to the highest degree.

Think on this for a minute. Imagine you could see beautiful

waves of light emanating from a pianist while he is lost in the reverie of his playing. Imagine you could see rays of light radiating from a person deep in meditation or in prayer. Now imagine yourself doing something that you love and those same glorious rays of light shining forth all around you.

Imagine someone shouting and swearing in a temper. They will be producing jagged waves, which jar all those around them. If you are living in an internal world of frustration and anger, you would also be giving off these frenetic energy patterns which are palpable to all those around you.

Ahimsa is learning to translate inner calm through your thoughts and tasks. When you work at an easy pace from a state of kindness, you will be in a state of grace. Remember the monk who washed his dishes with single-pointed focus? His main task wasn't the external one which could be seen but rather containment of the unseen internal world.

It can help to give a prayer to dedicate a task at the outset or to use affirmation while you work to continually remind yourself that ahimsa is the actual task at hand.

Prayer of non-violence

Dear father/mother/creator/God,
Please grant me the grace to sit quietly
within your great spirit,
as I face my daily challenges peacefully
and with a calm acceptance,
to neither harm others with my words, thoughts or actions
nor harm myself.
I pray that you may guide me in all that I do.
In deepest gratitude,
Amen.

Affirmations:
'I am at peace with myself.'
'I express harmony in all that I do.'

The light of the sun dwells within you
Welling up in bubbles of joy,
Lift the corners of your lips
And taste delight upon your tongue!

Oh how sweet this life is
When truth is beheld:
Shine on dear inner light
And illuminate us all.

Chapter 18

A better way to be

Thoughts are based either in love or fear. There is no other derivation. In this moment, and the next, and the next, thoughts percolate to the surface as unbidden visions (sometimes summoned from our own emotional attachment) but following a litany, a lineage if you like, based in either a fear or a love response.

Perhaps our strength as evolving humans is in recognising that we are drawn to *create* the next thought from that love/fear response. Our strength is in realising that we are becoming aware of that which was previously an unconscious process.

It is our choice to *create each moment*, each second, from love. Each second is a do-over. A chance to express love this time round. There is no need to wait for the perfect moment to come along because the moment is here and now. No need to start full of good intentions at a new year resolution, or the next new moon or even a fresh new morning. The good intentions start now, in this conscious moment. The creation of expression through love starts in this moment.

If you were God would you do any differently? That is my benchmark. For I believe that you are, we are, God. And choosing to act, think, breathe consciously from love is to act as God would act. To act in loving kindness towards others and in loving kindness most of all towards ourselves. Forgiving our own failings is often the hardest thing to achieve. It is far easier to forgive others; being able to see them from the viewpoint of the observer, we can understand why they might have acted the way they did. For we have all had moments when we could have done better, acted in a more forgiving, kindly way.

But towards ourselves, our judgements are often much more

harsh. That stops now.

Take this moment to affirm to yourself that you have acted always in the best way that you knew how at the time: you weren't always the wise and consciously thinking being that you are now. Your younger self chose how she/he did to the best of their understanding about life at that time. Be forgiving to your younger self. Pat yourself on the back for all that you did achieve well and for all the situations which you have faced with courage, integrity and tenacity. Hindsight is a great healer. Use that hindsight to let go of any harsh self-judgements. That unforgiving approach does not serve you or anyone else. We can't wear a hair shirt for all of eternity. Does punishing yourself really serve you? Or anyone else?

Imagine that you were able to give wise counsel to your younger self. What would you say? That you could have acted better? And would that help you now? Regret and guilt are based in fear responses.

If you were to act from love, what would love do? Forgiveness and acceptance are great levellers. I believe that you were always acting from the highest that you knew at the time. The fact that you know differently now is evidence that you have grown from the experience that life presented you with. Hindsight provides evidence that you *are* now an older and wiser version of yourself.

And you are still evolving. The more you consciously engage with your healing process, the more you are becoming enlightened. You will be able to contain more light, minute by minute, hour by hour.

Reflect in your journal on all the positive ways in which you have grown as a result of physical limitation. Think back to your younger self and how you may have acted in ways which you know in hindsight were not wise. How would you think, act and feel differently now?

Take yourself to your quiet meditation space. Ground into

the earth and place your protection around you.

Imagine that you are going back to a scene from your younger life. Your older and wiser self can walk in here and speak to him/her and give counsel. Keep your statements positive.

Remember that your approach to life then was limited. Viewing your past objectively can help you to understand why you acted in a particular way and help you to release judgement. Compassion and forgiveness follow understanding. Forgive your younger self. Imagine him/her smiling and feeling supported. Extend compassion towards him/her. Imagine laying down judgement and replacing it with Love.

Without judgement, connect with your younger self through a hug. Imagine him/her offloading their problems. Support him/her and give them the benefit of your present knowledge.

Reconnect your younger and present selves. Imagine them walking back to the waking world integrated and whole. Ground down any unwanted energy into the earth and re-visualise your protection.

Take the time to write your experiences in your journal.

I suggest that you accept the wiser you with gratitude. So as far as your health goes, you may see that your actions in the past have driven you to a state of imbalance and dis-ease. But you are not that person now. Life has allowed you the grace to grow into the wonderful being that you are now. Life flows beautifully in the next chapter of your life, with a grace and fresh under-standing of the nature of yourself. What a wonderful journey this has been! And it's not over yet!

So breathe in and breathe out with forgiveness and joy in all that is new and fresh in this moment.

You might like to affirm: *'I choose to remember who I am and to choose to act, think and be from a basis of love.'*

I am truly grateful for the magic that all of life's experiences had in store for me. What magical bonuses have you found inherent in each of the life experiences you've had? In especially the difficult challenges, kernels of truth and understanding are the richest. I like to remember that when faced with seemingly insurmountable odds. I feel an almost perverse excitement as I anticipate the wonder in store for me, even in the midst of disaster. I welcome change. The alternative is to fear it. But like King Canute, there is no stopping the tide of change anyway. Resisting change is futile and pointless, but worse it could halt our own spiritual progress and render that potentially rich learning experience presented in the guise of 'change' as null and void.

There are times in moments of dire hopelessness when you make a breakthrough in understanding the why of the illness translated into the greater why of existence itself. It is then that you realise that you are not this beleaguered body. If it ended its heartbeat now, you would not cease to exist. The truth is not *I breathe therefore I am* nor *I think therefore I am* but simply *I am, therefore I am*. And time falls away. In this final cessation of trying, something far greater takes place. You can experience a nothingness which paradoxically contains everything. A Zen moment. You touch the void. In this sublime mode of being, you are aware of only bliss, peace and life itself.

Identifying too closely and completely with the physicality of our bodies and this physical existence is folly. This physical world presents us with many falsehoods in order that we may come to know what truth is. You have come to appreciate what you have, only because you experienced lack. Sometimes when despair and hopelessness threatens to overwhelm us and we are literally out of our minds, we break through experience into pure existence beyond mind and body.

Decide to make a conscious choice to look for the glory and wonder of any of life's experiences. It's all part of life's rich tapestry. At the onset of Chronic Fatigue Syndrome, as my body stopped doing all except the most basic bodily functions, creativity didn't stop. It was simply re-channelled into new avenues. It started with words in my head, which for me, when I placed pen to paper, translated into wonderful stark poetry of a beauty, poignancy and clarity that I hitherto didn't know I possessed. Later, as I was recovering, I discovered that my new creativity extended as well to art.

I had created a new healthier lifestyle with a new diet, spending quiet mornings in reflection with my journal, schooling my thoughts, learning to pace my activity/rest periods, being as open and honest as possible with others, and forgiving myself from self-judgement. In creating this new me, my ability to detach from people and situations around me developed so that my inner strength grew. So much so that I became able to cope with most situations that I came up against.

To illustrate this, I would like to share a shamanic healing journey where I went to my inner garden. In meditation, I was disappointed to see that all the beds in my magical garden were barren and empty. There was a sculpted fountain, empty of water, with dead leaves in the dry grate. I found a giant tap beside the fountain and felt urged to turn it on. Out poured glorious life-giving water, filling the pool and spilling out into the flowerbeds which sprang to life and colour, spreading out as far as my eye could see. Rainbow-coloured fish spouted from the fountain and swam along in shoals between the avenues of flowers. It was a true Genesis moment.

I experienced an epiphany that, in an attempt to preserve my energy, I had turned my inner wellspring off. This may have worked for me as part of the healing process to stop me leaking energy, but as I became well, it was no longer appropriate. I am sharing that cathartic moment with you in the hope that you may recognise that, at some stage in recovery, you need to allow your energy to flow again without fear.

We will conclude with a meditation to create your inner garden. This is a representation of how well you are tending to and nurturing your inner spirit. You can 'turn on' your wellspring so that you have more energy in everyday life.

Meditation to tend your internal Garden of Creation
Breathe in white light, breathe out and release to the trees.

Ground and protect yourself.

In your imagination take yourself to your inner garden.

Notice the gate: is it well-oiled and rust-free?

Walk down the path and take note of the beds: are they well-tended or empty? Is the path overgrown or well-tended?

Walk to the centre of the garden, noting the condition of your garden.

There is a fountain in the centre of the garden: is it clean and well-kept? Note whether water is flowing, or is it dry?

Imagine there is a huge tap. Walk over and turn on the water. Observe what happens as your wellspring starts to flow.

If your garden requires tending, imagine you are sowing, watering, weeding or trimming.

In your inner garden, turn on the sunshine and make the conditions just right.

Stay for as long as you like, nurturing and being nurtured in your inner garden.

When you are ready to leave, walk back the way you came, closing the gate behind you.

Reaffirm your grounding and protection as you come back to wakefulness in your physical body.

Know that with every thought you are creating your reality around you. You can create anything you want! It's as easy as thinking and it's very powerful. Your reality is a heartbeat behind what you imagine it to be! How wonderful is that?

Time to get your Hogwarts' wand out and weave exactly what

you want in life. I bless you that your wellspring of life-giving energy will flow continuously and effortlessly until you recover total good health. Peace and blessings on you, fellow travellers on life's journey.

Affirmations:
'My life force flows effortlessly. I have unlimited energy.'
'I forgive and live in peace with myself.'

My favourite raw food recipes

I have included these recipes as a taster to whet your appetite towards raw, living food. These are all easy-peasy to make and delicious! Each recipe serves one person.

Breakfast: banana and blueberry smoothie

1 banana
1 handful of blueberries
1 tablespoon each of sunflower seeds, pumpkin seeds and raisins/sultanas
2 tablespoons linseed
5 or 6 nuts (brazils, almond, hazelnuts, pecans...)
½ mug of nut milk (or use a bought carton of vegan milk)
Whizz and enjoy.

NB: I tend to vary this basic recipe by adding ingredients such as maca root powder (for energy!), vanilla essence, a kale leaf, hemp or wheatgrass powder or spirulina powder. All of these supplements are superfoods. Or try swapping banana for mango, and blueberries for other soft fruits as they come into season. Play with the basic recipe until you have a smoothie that you love. It's a brilliant kick-start of energy to your day!

Make your own almond milk
Soak half a cup of nuts (almonds or brazils) in cold water overnight.
Drain and discard the water. This removes heavier toxins from nuts so that they are easier to digest.
Place in your blender jug with 2 cups of fresh cold water.

Blend for 3 minutes.

Drain the liquid through a sieve into a bowl.

Place the pulp back in the blender jug with another cup of water. Blend for 3 minutes and drain again (in order to get more 'milk' from the nuts a second time). Your nut milk is now ready to use. Keep in a fridge for up to 3 days.

NB: you can use the leftover nut pulp to make the 'almond crackers' below.

Lunch: miso soup with almond crackers

Miso soup

5 small or 2 large tomatoes

1 tablespoon raw miso paste

3 mushrooms

½ teaspoon sea salt or pink Himalayan salt

½ sheet of nori seaweed

½ cup of boiling water (allow to cool slightly)

Blend for 2 minutes, pour and enjoy.

Almond crackers

Place the nut pulp (left over from nut milk) in the blender with:

½ red pepper

1 clove of garlic

½ cup of golden linseed

1 tablespoon of olive oil

½ teaspoon sea salt (or pink Himalayan salt)

1 teaspoon dried herbs

Blend for 4 minutes. Spread the paste out on an oiled baking sheet or baking parchment.

Dehydrate for 6 hours in the oven at the lowest setting with the door slightly open to ensure that the temperature doesn't rise above 50 °C. Turn these over after 3 hours to dehydrate the other side.

When the crackers are no longer sticky, remove from the baking sheet. They will store for 30 days in the fridge.

Evening meal: 'roast' vegetables, vegan coleslaw with cashew mayonnaise and salad

'Roast' vegetables
1 courgette

2 peppers (any colour)

3 tomatoes

3 or 4 mushrooms

2oz olive oil

1 clove garlic

1 teaspoon dried herbs or ½ cup fresh basil

½ teaspoon sea salt or Himalayan salt

Peel and thickly slice all vegetables and place on a baking sheet. Place the oil, garlic, herbs and salt in the blender for 1 minute. Pour over the vegetables. Dehydrate in the oven at the lowest setting for 2 hours with the door ajar.

Vegan coleslaw
¼ red cabbage, thinly sliced

1 kale leaf, cut into thin strips

1 carrot, peeled and grated (or try a parsnip)

2 pineapple rings, diced

5 chopped almonds

3 tablespoons sesame seeds

Toss in a bowl with cashew mayonnaise.

Cashew mayonnaise
½ cup sunflower oil

1 teaspoon mustard seeds

½ lemon, juiced

3 tablespoons organic cider vinegar

¾ cup of nut milk

½ cup of cashew nuts

½ teaspoon sea salt or Himalayan salt

Blend until smooth. If the mixture is too thin, add five more nuts and blend. If it still too thin, add ¼ teaspoon xanthan gum and blend.

This mayonnaise can be stored in the fridge for up to 5 days.

Salad

Try to use a variety of green leaves. Our palate needs to taste bitter as well as sweet to ensure that we get all the minerals we require. Try using raw kale, cut into strips, in a salad. Interesting additions are to pick dandelion leaves or hairy bitter cress from your garden as these 'weeds' will grow all year round.

A favourite of mine is to place sliced grapefruit or orange on a bed of leaves and sprinkle with sunflower and sesame seeds.

Appendix B

(you may photocopy and enlarge this chart)

14-day sleep diary

	Mid-night	1	2	3	4	5	6	7	8	9	10	11	12 noon	1	2	3	4	5	6	7	8	9	10	11
Mon																								
Tues																								
Wed																								
Thurs																								
Fri																								
Sat																								
Sun																								
Mon																								
Tues																								
Wed																								
Thurs																								
Fri																								
Sat																								
Sun																								

Bibliography

Chapter 8: Sensitivity to sound and ELF (extremely low frequencies of electromagnetic energy)

Jenny, Hans. *Kymatik: Wellen und Schwingungen mit ihrer Struktur und Dynamik/Cymatics* (The Structure and Dynamics of Waves and Vibrations), 1967, Basilius Press, p. 10.

Maisch, D., Rapley, B., Rowland, R.E., Podd, J. 'Chronic Fatigue Syndrome: Is Prolonged Exposure to Environmental Level Powerline Frequency Electromagnetic Fields a Co-Factor to Consider in Treatment?' *Journal of the Australasian College of Nutritional & Environmental Medicine*, Vol. 17, No. 2, December 1998, pages 29–35.

Chapter 11: The raw food diet

Virtue, Doreen and Ross, Jenny. *The Art of Raw, Living Food*, 2009, Hay House; ISBN 978-1-401-92183-5.

Myhill, S., Booth, N.E., McLaren-Howard, J. 'Chronic Fatigue Syndrome and Mitochondrial Dysfunction.' *International Journal of Clinical and Experimental Medicine*, 2009, 2:1–16.

http://igennus.com/health-conditions/chronic-fatigue-syndrome-symptoms

Chapter 13: Arrhythmia: the message of the heart

Cooper, Diana. *A Little Light on the Spiritual Laws*, 2000, Hodder and Stoughton, Mobius; ISBN 978-0-340-83508-1.

Chapter 14: Meaning of the illness

Friedman, M., & Rosenman, R.H. (1959). 'Association of Specific Overt Behavior Pattern with Blood and Cardiovascular Findings Blood: Cholesterol Level, Blood Clotting Time, Incidence of Arcus Senilis, and Clinical Coronary Artery Disease.' *Journal of the American Medical Association*, 169(12),

1286–1296.
Shepherd, Charles. *Living with M.E.: The Chronic/Post-Viral Fatigue Syndrome*, 3rd edn, 1999, Vermilion, Random House Publishers, London; IBSN 0-09-181679-3.

Chapter 16: Other therapies and supplements
Shepherd, Charles. *Living with M.E.: The Chronic/Post-Viral Fatigue Syndrome*, 3rd edn, 1999, Vermilion, Random House Publishers, London; IBSN 0-09-181679-3.
'Clinical nutrition for chronic fatigue syndrome/myalgic encephalomyelitis'
http://igennus.com/wp-content/uploads/2014/03/Nutrition-education-series_CFS.pdf

About the author

Jenny Light is an intuitive, inspirational speaker, therapist, teacher of meditation and yoga, healer and artist. She lives in Ayrshire, Scotland.

Jenny runs many courses and events, and is available for one-to-one support.

www.living-lightly.co.uk

AYNI
BOOKS

"Ayni" is a Quechua word meaning "reciprocity" – sharing, giving and receiving – whatever you give out comes back to you. To be in Ayni is to be in balance, harmony and right relationship with oneself and nature, of which we are all an intrinsic part. Complementary and Alternative approaches to health and well-being essentially follow a holistic model, within which one is given support and encouragement to move towards a state of balance, true health and wholeness, ultimately leading to the awareness of one's unique place in the Universal jigsaw of life – Ayni, in fact.